ADVANCE PRAISE FOR SKILL

"After dissecting this book by Chris Ahmad, MD, I was first puzzled by its purpose. As I read further, I began to realize the uniqueness of this book which is unlike any other that I have come across!

"To some extent it is a motivational book built on common sense and based on the personal experiences of its author. On the other side of the coin, there is sophistication of its content.

"The book gives you a step by step framework for success and greatness! Another unique perspective is that it doesn't matter what your occupation is it speaks to us all!

"The central core of this book comprises 40 principles that can allow the reader to reach his/her greatest potential!

"I would agree with this book's very talented author that you are never God's Gift to anything—you have to work for it!

"Most of the book demonstrates that if you want to individually be successful and reach mastery, it is solely left up to you and how you apply yourself."

Dr. James Andrews
Co-Founder, American Sports Medicine Institute (ASMI)
Co-Founder, Andrews Sports Medicine and Orthopaedic Center

"As a pediatric spine surgeon, I can attest to the universal power and truth contained in these pages which should be a must read for any physician, and really anyone looking to perfect their craft. In *Skill*, Ahmad artfully dissects the critical underpinnings of Mastery. This short book will make you more thoughtful and more skilled—whether your goal is surgical excellence, athletics or simply self understanding."

Michael Vitale MD MPH
Ana Lucia Professor of Pediatric Orthopaedic Surgery
Columbia University Medical Center
Co-Director, Division of Pediatric Orthopaedics
Chief Quality Officer, Department of Orthopaedic Surgery
Chief, Pediatric Spine and Scoliosis Service
Medical Director, MSCH Initiative to "Make Care Better"
Morgan Stanley Childrens Hospital of New York—Presbyterian

"Everyone is interested in learning how to improve their skill level and how a leading surgeon with engineering training approaches skill development. The short chapters of SKILL are fun and engaging. They make you want to read to the next chapter. The summary statements are deft and memorable.

"How good would surgeons be if they practiced their hand/eye skills as frequently as a professional golfer does, with teachers and a practice, practice, practice work ethic?

"I hope this book opens eyes to this overwhelming challenge."

Reinhold Schmieding
Founder & President, Arthrex Inc.

SKILL

**40 PRINCIPLES
THAT SURGEONS,
ATHLETES, AND OTHER
ELITE PERFORMERS USE
TO ACHIEVE MASTERY**

SKILL

CHRISTOPHER S. AHMAD, MD

LP

LEAD PLAYER

NEW YORK

Lead Player LLC

To reach the author or Lead Player LLC,
email: info@chrisahmadmd.com

ISBN: 978-0-9963885-0-4

Digital editions available.

First Edition

Cover and book design: John Lotte for Meryl Moss Media
merylmossmedia.com

www.chrisahmadmd.com

This book is for everyone who's inspired and supported me with hope that it inspires and supports others.

I found the structure, ideas and value for this book in Dan Coyle's words. And I live by them.

Debating and exploring life with Ken Shubin Stein keeps me energized, focused and on my toes.

My brother Greg has been my deepest source of inspiration.

My parents Shafi and Judy have been a guiding light for me for my entire life.

My wife Beth and children Charlie, Sofie, and Brady encourage and challenge me every day and everything I do is for them.

I am not gifted . . .

TABLE OF CONTENTS

PART ONE: DEFINING SKILLS

PART TWO: IMPROVING SKILLS

Deep training—Find the sweet spot, then reach and repeat. *45*

PART THREE: ACHIEVING MASTERY

Develop motivation, grit, and analytical honesty *89*

PART FOUR: ADDITIONAL REFLECTIONS

FOREWORD BY DAN COYLE

I remember the first time I met Christopher Ahmad. It was June 2013 at Yankee Stadium before a game. We met in an oak-paneled restaurant filled with gleaming photos of Babe Ruth, Mickey Mantle, Joe DiMaggio, and other legends. At first glance, Ahmad fit in with that storied lineup, perhaps as a leadoff hitter. He was impossibly young, impossibly bright, and impossibly skilled, having become the team's head physician during what, by all appearances, must have been his early teens. The facts seemed clear: Dr. Christopher Ahmad was a prodigy, a breed apart, gifted to a level beyond expectation or logic. (His CV runs *51 pages*.) I would not have been particularly shocked if Ahmad had suddenly unpeeled his suit coat, grabbed a baseball glove, and jogged out to play centerfield.

Then I read Ahmad's book. That's when the true nature of his gifts became apparent. Because Ahmad didn't start out as a super-talented surgeon—he became one. He built his skills, one by one, through a creative and concentrated training process that rivals that of any of the athletes for whom he cares. And one of those skills, to our good fortune, is his ability to clearly relate how that process worked for him, and how it might work for others.

Traditionally, the medical establishment has approached surgical training in roughly the same way that the Department of Motor Vehicles approaches driver education: there's a series of exams followed by a long, indefinite, unsupervised period of on-the-job learning, during which the improvement process is largely left up to the initiative of the learner and the circumstances of fate. The model Ahmad offers us is vastly different. It resembles the deliberate training of a modern athlete, and uses targeted, active methods aligned with the process that underlies all improvement: getting to the edge of your ability, reaching just beyond it, and paying deep attention to your mistakes. Instead of being the passive recipient of knowledge, the trainee becomes an active builder of their skills.

There was a time, not so many years ago, when I dreamed of becoming a doctor. I majored in pre-medical studies, got good grades, and even took the MCAT before making an 11th-hour turn to my other love, writing. I've often pondered why I switched paths, and here is my answer: I was attracted to writing because it felt like a specific, concrete skill I could practice and master, while medicine seemed towering and mysterious, a world populated by demigods and geniuses. But reading this book has made me wonder what life would have been like if I had chosen the medical path. Not just because Ahmad is a good writer or a skilled surgeon, but rather because it makes me feel that thrilling emotion that will be felt by every person who reads it, a warm, energizing feeling that if translated into words would be something like: *Hey, I could do that!*

Daniel Coyle
New York Times best-selling author of *The Talent Code*

INTRODUCTION

Watching a truly talented surgeon manipulate a scalpel can be like watching Tom Brady orchestrate a touchdown drive, or LeBron James driving to the hoop and, in split seconds, change the course of a game. Some surgeons calmly bring high-speed motor vehicle accident victims back to life, and some surgeons precisely fashion elbow ligament reconstructions enabling MLB pitchers with $100 million contracts to exceed their pre-injury pitch velocity. Mysterious talents exist in surgeons that are similar to the unique magic of athletes, musicians, and chess players.

I have dedicated myself to elite-level surgical skill development since my first year as an undergraduate mechanical engineering student at Columbia University. I believed the greatest engineering wonders occurred in the human body, which led me to pursue a career in orthopaedic surgery. I was captured by the intensity and thrilling precision required of surgeons performing under the pressure of error consequences that risk life or lifelong morbidity. At times, I believed surgeons had talent with unreachable capabilities—when compared to me—equal to a young kid watching his professional athlete idol perform.

While many elite surgeons are indeed considered gifted, or born with talent, I engaged in a life-long pursuit of surgical excellence, ignoring the notion that skill would plateau, or a low dose of natural talent would limit my growth. It became my passion to unlock potential. My mission was to perform surgery with extreme proficiency, similar to World Cup leading goal scorers, and develop new surgical procedures that would preserve the dreams of patients aspiring to play in the World Cup. Now, in my 12th year practicing orthopaedic surgery at Columbia University, I maintain an intense medical practice where I treat sports injuries and complex conditions involving the shoulder, elbow, and knee in recreational and professional athletes. I am, perhaps, most tested with managing the health of the New York Yankees as their head team physician. I am also challenged with training surgical skill to orthopaedic residents and fellows. My journey now has brought me to the level of chief of sports medicine and vice chairman of research at Columbia University. I have also participated in more than 250 scientific articles related to surgical technique, and authored four surgical textbooks.

Like all surgeons, I am deeply fulfilled by my technical surgical abilities that encompass a complex balance of reproducible hard skills and improvisational soft skills. I consciously developed strategies to maximize my own personal surgical mastery and also educate and facilitate skill development in young surgeons in training. I created these strategies, which I now regard as my greatest asset, by successfully adapting skills I discovered in my adolescence playing soccer in college, and playing guitar recreationally. As a preadolescent athlete, I applied deep practice principles with relentless motivation and grit tested under pressured competitions. To my surprise, these self-learned principles have become scientifically proven to enhance skill and form the strategy I continue to use today.

I shared these personal strategies during late evening conversations with my brother-in-law and friend Dr. Kenneth Shubin Stein, who maintains similar interests in financial and business mastery. Ken had recently sent me a copy of *The Little Book of Talent,* written by Daniel Coyle. I discovered a terrific manual containing 53 very general "Tips" that, with little effort, I transformed into highly specific tips directly applied to surgical skill development.

I started a process where, every evening, I converted one of Coyle's general tips directly to my surgical skill development, synthesizing Coyle's research and proven methods with my own personal strategies that I established over the course of several decades. Within two months, I found

I had created a document that has shaped my ongoing quest for surgical excellence. I further expanded on specific features that enhance performance to complete the manual. It also became apparent that sharing this product may help others in their pursuit for excellence—surgical, artistic, athletic, or commercial.

I hope this benefits any individual who wishes to convert general proven principles of skill acquisition to highly specific endeavors (managing a business, such as Coca-Cola's Chairman and CEO Muhtar Kent; playing tournament chess like Bobby Fischer; parenting remarkably like my wife; lowering a golf handicap like my brother, or cooking like a five-star restaurant chef—my hobby).

HOW TO USE THIS BOOK

While many talented surgeons deep into their careers demonstrate what is perceived as *natural* talent, many of these surgeons do not clearly grasp why or how they achieved their level of skill. I believe the true magic of these "naturally talented surgeons" can be traced to highly specialized skill development techniques. Those who lack "natural talents" can create those environments and, thereby, manufacture talent. Furthermore, surgery requires a career dedication of lifelong mastery techniques. It would surprise many patients to know that many advanced surgeons regularly use as little as 10 percent of the surgery learned during their training, where their competence was built, because of the continuously advancing nature of medicine.

The most highly skilled surgeons, therefore, embrace the *process* where skill development is employed continuously throughout one's career and not simply to start a career. For many occupations, accepted principles are that training can take 10 years, practice goes on for 30 years, and then retirement completes the career. Medicine and surgery, in contrast, require constant continuous training—a feature that attracts many with such appetites. Despite historical learning trajectories, there isn't a profession or avocation that won't benefit from the same dedication to constant training and re-mastery of one's skills and experiences.

LEARNING TO PUSH BOUNDARIES

As my learning evolved, I have specialized in performing specific operations such as Tommy John Surgery[1] that enables professional pitchers to throw upwards of 100 mph and arthroscopic shoulder stabilization surgery that allows gymnasts to vault violently without fear of dislocating their shoulder. I am able to do these things because I never stop practicing, stretching, and searching for deeper and more formidable boundaries.

This book is intended for those who seek mastery and are interested in taking basic principles of talent acquisition created and employed by one surgeon, and applying them to their own personal and specific quest. Forty tips demonstrate how to begin, execute, and sustain mastery. As you read through the tips, imagine how to incorporate them directly to your journey. Incorporating these tips into your life will clear the path to growth and mastery in specific domains for those who take it.

While I do not consider myself gifted, I've come to realize that the real gifts are contained in several simple tips included in this book.

PART ONE:
DEFINING SKILLS

1

Don't fall for the prodigy myth. People outside of medicine, especially those who are squea-
mish about blood, can be awestruck by surgeons.
The simple magnificence of a surgeon working
with only his hands and a tray of instruments
who can reconfigure a four-month-old's mal-
formed heart—a child who was otherwise des-
tined to die, but goes on to live a healthy life and
even excel in sports—creates an aura of mys-
tery. Performing with extreme surgical skill in-
vokes the "God-given talent" theory—similar to
how we explain Tiger Woods, Itzhak Perlman, or
Leonardo DaVinci. But to have the skill to modify
the workings of the human body—changing the
course of life—that must be a God-given gift.

For those familiar with surgery and surgical
training, it becomes awkwardly apparent that
some surgeons are okay at what they do, many
are competent, and a select few exceed the average with mystical superiority. Most surgeons in
training easily can appreciate a talented surgeon
as compared to an average or below average surgeon. Their procedures are performed with a

calmness, flow, and beauty as lyrical as a musical performance.

Some young surgeons believe that perhaps the super-talented have a foundation of exceptional intelligence or huge memories, or other gifts which give them a competitive edge. It can actually be cognitively pleasing for the middle-bell-curve population to attribute those with talent as having inherited a gift. "God didn't bless me with good hands, therefore, I am not responsible for my failure to achieve greatness."

Research, personal experience, and even common sense argue otherwise—and convincingly. First, consider that early success often does not predict long-term success. Countless top performers were overlooked early: Michael Jordan cut from his high school varsity team as a sophomore; Walt Disney criticized early for lack of imagination. Others include Albert Einstein, Winston Churchill, and Lucille Ball. In fact, those who enjoy early success may be disadvantaged because they often attempt to protect their achievements by risking little, which stops their progression.

Prodigies are hard, if not impossible, to identify early in their path to greatness. Coaches at the Olympic training center in Colorado Springs appreciate this and, when asked, "Could you predict in two years who would win a Gold Medal?" Only one out of 50 responded "Yes," indicating that early prediction is poor. Anson Dorrance, head coach of North Carolina's women's soccer

team with an incredible 21 national championships, says, "One of the most unfortunate things
I see when identifying youth players is the girl
who is told over the years how great she is. By
the time she's a high school freshman, she starts
to believe it. By her senior year, she's fizzled out.
Then there's her counterpart: the girl waiting in
the wings who quietly and with determination
decides she's going to make something of herself.
Invariably, this humble, hard-working girl is the
one who becomes the real player."

Observational research explains that a process leads to greatness. Dan Coyle in *The Talent
Code* observed that a Russian tennis club with
a single indoor court has created more top-20
women players than the United States; that
Brazil has more professional soccer players; that
the Dominican Republic now accounts for one in
nine MLB baseball players. These observations
now can be explained.

Tiger Woods' success also can be explained.
His father, Earl Woods, was a tremendous
teacher with experience teaching military history and tactics at the City College of New York,
and playing high school and college baseball. His
son, Tiger, was from a second marriage, and the
three children from his first marriage already
were grown. He was retired, and was dedicated
to the training of a Tiger, who had a putter in his
hand at seven months and watched Earl hit while
sitting in his high chair. Before age two, he was
practicing at the golf course. By age four, he had

professional teachers. By 19, he was considered an elite player and had summed up 17 years of intense practice. Similar child prodigies, such as Mozart, Gary Kasparov, Jet Li and many others, have training that explains their gifts.

The bottom line is that talent, in any field, is created through specific tools . . . not simple experience, not in-born abilities, not even memory or intelligence. Don't fall for the convenient argument, "How do we explain great performance and its rarity? With natural talent, the talented effortlessly can do things that others never will be able to do." The reality, however, as science and personal experience will demonstrate, is that supreme surgical skill is in the hands of the surgeon, not the gods—as are all great talents.

Talent is not bestowed; find out how to get yours.

2

It's not the environment. It's you. Some

feel they never achieve greatness because they were not blessed by God. Some feel a poor performance was caused by the environment they were placed in and imply they have no control. Simply stated, poor performers with no future say things such as, "The coach doesn't like me," or "The weather was too cold for me to get loose." If you find yourself making excuses for your performance, you are in big trouble.

I have friends who search the internet for the ideal golf club to enable them to drive the ball more accurately and with more distance. But equipment can only take you so far. I recall hearing of a young surgeon who performed a complicated ankle operation. The ankle required an external fixator. An "ex-fix" is a device that requires fixing threaded pins into the bones above and below the ankle that are then attached together like an erector set. It stabilizes the ankle and keeps the shattered bones in good position and reduces stress on the soft tissues. Postoperatively, however, the surgeon noticed the patient's foot was paralyzed. The reason was that one of the ex-fix pins penetrated the nerve that controls the foot. The surgeon concluded that the fixator was poorly designed.

Athletes often blame referees for a poor performance. Some even blame teammates. The most elite surgeons, athletes, and leaders take responsibility for their action and create an environment to improve their future.

Your first step toward mastery is accepting responsibility.

3

Reverse engineer your mentor. Every

surgeon has been sparked by a mentor or a role
model who ignited his or her interest in surgical excellence. I expect this is true of everyone
who participates in a profession or avocation
they care deeply about. This ignition is strikingly
similar to talent hotbeds observed in sports or
music. I grew up playing soccer with dreams of
scoring goals in a World Cup match. Like many
kids, I had posters on my bedroom wall of the
world's top players—Pele, Franz Beckenbauer,
and Carlos Alberto. And, similar to many kids,
I stared at their photos and mimicked them in
my backyard while wearing a jersey with the
number 10 on it.

Perhaps different from some kids, I went beyond the simple sense of awe these elite players
evoked. I studied them and constructed in a notebook the features I believed made them exceptional. I truly dissected them: Pele: speed, agility,
goal-scoring sense; Franz Beckenbauer: composure, creativity, improvisation; Carlos Alberto:
physical presence, leadership, confidence.

Reverse engineering is a process that takes apart an object to see how it works to duplicate or enhance the object. I planned out strategic practice sessions to replicate the remarkable features of the world's best. I recall frustrating practice sessions where I had poor concentration or limited motivation, or simply was tired from a prior workout. Rather than pack it in and call it a day with a lost practice opportunity, I would go home and watch a video of a historic great game: a World Cup match in black and white with George Best playing for England with ball handling domination; or the Brazil World Cup match with Pele scoring goals at age 17. Usually within 30 minutes, I would experience a new energy and enthusiasm and was pressing the TV's off switch and was back in my Jeep heading to the high school with 20 soccer balls and revived focus to master the moves I just observed.

During medical school, I had a photo on the back wall of my desk depicting a surgeon operating with surgical loops and hands deep in a wound, manipulating delicate instruments. I subscribed to the *Journal of Bone and Joint Surgery* (the prestigious journal read by all orthopaedic surgeons) as a medical student. I would thumb through the journal, read research articles, and began recognizing the academic leaders of orthopaedic surgery and sports medicine.

During my own residency training at Columbia, I dissected the qualities of each of my mentors and explored the origins of their excellence: composure under pressure, work ethic, anatomical knowledge, biomechanics expertise, management of patients with misguided perceptions, fanatic discipline, and superior judgment. I have had many surgeons inspire me, those who never panic in the most dire situations; others who have a technical proficiency converting crazy-difficult surgeries into casual procedures.

Identify those surgeon(s), mentors, or heroes who have inspired you and watch them closely. Do not passively observe them. Take command and immerse yourself in their excellence. Dan Coyle has observed talent hot beds of music and sports where the world's top performers are produced. Learners at these centers spend time observing top performers, staring with an intensely unblinking gaze. The walls of these hotbeds are cluttered with photos and posters of their stars.

When I was a kid, I bought the same brand soccer cleats that Pele wore. Now, I wear the same brand surgical gloves of my surgical mentors. At the end of the day, it's not about the equipment though (although it can't hurt); it's about identifying, breaking down, absorbing, and figuring out how to implement the qualities that feed excellence.

Dissect your mentor and flatter him or her with sincere imitation.

4

Seek out and steal pearls. Orthopaedic surgery is comprised of numerous delicate skills, such as untangling a nerve from a bed of scar tissue, or creating multiple precise tunnels in bone that connect perfectly while not weakening the overall strength of the bone. The flow and sequence replicate a musician's moves and can mimic a magician sequentially performing the elements of his illusion. The first step in learning surgical tricks is to *steal* them. Some surgical residents-in-training passively wait for principles to be bestowed upon them. It's more efficient to search and steal. I regularly email myself "ideas" the instant I see a new surgical trick. These ideas or tricks make it into my archived notes for later review and incorporation into my surgical toolbox.

I recently had an opportunity to observe a world expert perform a live demonstration of a shoulder labral repair surgery where he demonstrated a suture passing technique new to me. I sent an email to myself from my phone. Later that week, I reviewed the technique, studied it intensely, and then performed the exact technique on a high school football player suffering from shoulder dislocations. The new technique worked better than what I was formerly doing.

I recently observed an elbow expert present his 25 years of experience doing Tommy John surgery. I recorded it with my phone, then listened to it with earplugs while I transcribed it. I read the transcription before my next five Tommy John surgeries to improve my technique.

I catalogue multiple Word files with names such as "shoulder stabilization notes" or "ACL reconstruction notes." I use this same technique even outside of surgery—for example, I have a file called "public speaking notes." I attended a presentation given by Kenneth Cole and was impressed with how he locked in his audience with a clever story of how he sold his first pair of shoes. I emailed the anecdote to myself. I was later asked to give the keynote address at the last Columbia University Soccer Annual Alumni Banquet, and I used his story with my own improvisation. It worked beautifully. I file notes and review them on a regular basis. I use the ideas of others to stimulate my own new ideas.

Young boys and girls across America and, in fact, around the world, enjoy replicating Derek Jeter's approach to the plate—right hand in the air with his left foot out of the batter's box, step in with left foot, give a head nod, and then swing a few times while squinting at the pitcher. Young athletes mimic those qualities and, with maturity, stylize them to make them their own. If a technique you are stealing is practiced enough to become automatic, you can then free your own creativity, and modify the technique to make it more useful to you. So, why don't surgeons steal more often? Why don't surgeons take notes while at lectures? Stealing to benefit patients is not morally repulsive. It is rather that changing or adapting a new approach requires effort and sweat. Stop passively observing excellence and start stealing tools and techniques that create excellence—regardless of your profession.

Sam Walton, the respected business tycoon who created the powerhouse company Walmart, is famous for observing the practices of other companies and implementing them to his advantage. "I probably have traveled and walked into more variety stores than anybody in America. I am just trying to get ideas, any kind of ideas, that will help our company. Most of us don't invent ideas. We take the best ideas from someone else," said Walton. As described in the book *Decisive: How to Make Better Choices in Life and Work* by Chip and Dan Heath, Sam Walton was running a variety store in Bentonville, Arkansas. As he scoured other stores for better ideas, he learned that a Ben Franklin variety store in Minnesota had created a new and perhaps improved approach to the checkout line. Walton hopped on a bus and made the 600-mile trek to Pipestone, Minnesota. He was immediately impressed with a style of single, centralized checkout at the front of the store. This departed from the industry norm of departmental checkouts. In most stores, including Walton's own, customers shopping for dishwashing soap would pay at the kitchen counter and if they also needed hand soap, they'd pay separately at the toiletries counter.

Walton recognized the centralized model had several key advantages, such as fewer checkout clerks and higher customer convenience and satisfaction. Walton quickly implemented the technique in his own stores and Walmart continues to use the same model today. "Most everything I've done I've copied from someone else," said Walton.

Ideas can be copied precisely or conceptually. The current-day strategy for Amazon Prime copies Wal-Mart's concept, but executes it differently. Customers who sign up for Prime can then "one-click" items for free delivery to their delivery destinations. The efficiency and customer satisfaction of the e-mart checkout was so greatly improved that customers spent as much as 150 percent more at Amazon after they became Prime members.

I don't just steal other surgeon's ideas and incorporate them into my own practice; I steal my own concepts and re-apply them in areas that have not been previously considered. As an example, my exhaustive study of Tommy John surgery, that allows pitchers to come back following elbow ligament injury, led me to apply that exact surgical strategy to correct a torn ligament in the knee to stop a patella from dislocating. The "docking procedure," as it is called for the elbow, now has a "docking procedure" for patella ligament reconstruction. This knee procedure is now performed by many surgeons around the country.

Steal it, work it into your toolbox, and then modify it to create your own enduring personal skill.

5

Engrave your favorite procedure into your brain.

A favorite question I pose to medical students who apply for a position in our orthopaedic residency, and current residents on my service who work directly with me, is: "What is your favorite operation?"

In October 2000, I assisted Dr. Frank Jobe perform an elbow MCL reconstruction (Tommy John surgery, which Dr. Jobe invented) on a professional pitcher. I immediately transcribed the procedure to paper. This process of writing technical details began the process of mentally archiving the steps and important features. I would go back and study my notes as if I were preparing for a written test. I would close my eyes and mentally mimic the steps of the surgery. I projected myself onto his stool (the operation is performed sitting on stools) repeatedly.

I do recall that, as I studied him intensely for the first surgery we performed together, he looked at me and said, "How about I try this one left-handed?" I was utterly amazed with his

confidence as he split the skin overlying the inside aspect of the elbow with a scalpel gripped
in his left hand until I got the joke (he is, and always has been, left-handed). Every MCL reconstruction case that I assisted with thereafter,
I challenged myself to come up with at least five
"pearls" or new take-away points to improve my
understanding.

I have since performed several hundred MCL
reconstructions on patients of both amateur
and professional skill levels, written more than
100 articles related to aspects of MCL reconstructive surgery, and have given more than 100 presentations related to this operation. I even gave a
seminar on elbow MCL reconstruction to an audience of surgeons in combination with Tommy
John himself, who recounted to the audience his
experience as a patient. I continue to go back to
my original, step-by-step notes and the original
drawings. While surgery evolves with improvements, surgeons often have the deepest understanding from the mental blueprints of their
historical experience that they then work from.
Dr. Frank Jobe is considered by many worthy of
induction into the Baseball Hall of Fame for this
work.

If you are a surgeon, declare your favorite operation. Once you have developed expertise and
confidence with true mastery in that particular
operation, you will be in a position to expand
your mastery to other, similar, operations.

Surgery and music are similar in this regard. Musicians consistently continue to embrace the most challenging piece they struggled to learn early in their development. They pounded at it until they got it. Years later, and throughout their careers, they continue to play it. They use the experience in two ways: 1) Learning the method to master something triggers an enormous enthusiasm to reach for even more mastery, 2) Mastery of one technique requires developing specific tools that can be used in other ways.

To transfer this concept to surgery: if you understand all the nuances and subtleties of passing a soft tissue graft for Tommy John surgery, passing grafts for a surgery such as ACL reconstruction, or doing a biceps tendon repair, becomes easy.

If you are a writer, what is your favorite manuscript? If you are a chess player, what was your favorite historical game? If you are a chef, what is your favorite recipe?

Perfect your favorite endeavor, and use the skills you learned to master something harder.

———————

6

Always carry a notebook. High-level performers keep a performance journal (in addition to a stolen item journal from tip #3). They write and reflect. I began with marble composition books that I brought to the OR. I then changed to spiral notebooks with perforated sheets that I would tear out and organize by subject matter in three-ring binders. My typical notes look like, "For maximal exposure on the underface of the patella for a cartilage resurfacing procedure—place a single pin in the patella and use it as a joy stick. Great control of patella position for exposure."

Notes on surgical skill make up 70 percent of all my notes, but recently, notes on other aspects of sports medicine have been increasing in volume. For example, because I was compelled after Yankee games to take notes on the care I rendered to pinstripe players during the game, I purchased an electronic Dictaphone. I typically leave an evening game at 11 p.m. and it takes thirty minutes to get to the West Side Highway and then my apartment on the Lower West Side.

I dictate the experiences of the game and then use Dragon software to transcribe the notes. They then get filed on my computer. I reflect honestly on the strengths and weaknesses of that day's game coverage and plan for tomorrow's improvement. I review my notes regularly. I keep an ongoing journal of each type of surgery and put in new entries. I have transitioned from the use of a composition book to electronic files and have easy access to them wherever and whenever I want them.

Being a team physician can be extremely rewarding, but what is under appreciated and overlooked are the challenges behind the scenes, such as informing a player that he is injured, may miss the season, or may even have ended his career. I have presented devastating injury news to countless players over the years. Early on, I felt extremely uncomfortable with delivering bad news to an athlete. Patients were devastated and I felt I was not doing as good a job as I could. I decided to write down my approach to delivering news and then reflect on improving my methods.

On a cold day in October playoff baseball, our team captain Derek Jeter grabbed a routine ground ball and twisted to throw to first base, something fans have watched him do routinely for 20 years. This play, he collapsed to the ground with an expression of horrible pain. He was carried off the field to see me in the training room. I examined him and obtained x-rays immediately. The x-rays showed a fracture in his ankle. We were in the playoffs. He was the captain.

I returned from the x-ray room to where he was lying on a treatment table in the training room. It was time to deliver the results and what it would mean. When I stood next to him, he was surrounded by Yankee General Manager Brian Cashman, Joe Torre, who was visiting, Joe Girardi, Tino Martinez, who was at the game, and Reggie Jackson. I wrote down how I delivered the news that day and am still replaying how to improve upon it. This process holds for all surgical procedures or any area in which I am trying to improve or excel.

I learned from analysis that players fear not being able to play, and their biggest fear is that their career is over or compromised. For a player such as Derek Jeter who has, in the past, pushed through pain and injury to keep playing, I began the delivery with, "You are injured, and you will not be able to play through this injury." After it sunk in for a moment, I then explained, "Your career is not over by any means." Reflecting on delivery of injury news shaped the approach I used that day, so now I can do it without even having to think about it.

After reflecting on many notes, I decided to take an approach that would allow patients to understand their situation, and give them hope by using examples of others who have had the same injury and returned. I wanted to leave them with a mental picture of them playing again.

For the holidays each year, I purchase leather notebooks and give them to my orthopaedic surgical fellows. I inscribe on the inside, "Write your results from today, ideas for tomorrow, goals for next week. Create your map with the destination of surgical excellence." When I was a resident and fellow, I wrote down—in detail—the steps of each surgical case I assisted in, using my composition book I drew pictures of the anatomical structures, and numbered the sequence of suture passing with as much detail as possible. I would document it immediately after the surgery while my memory was fresh.

> **My notebook is one of my most private and prized possessions. (I also have notebooks on cooking, chess tactics, and wine.)**

———

7

Write down goals and commit to the process.

Creating appropriate goals is essential to advancement. Some surgeons fall short by failing to create objective goals. Average surgeons have goals, but often lack specifics or a formulated process to achieve those goals. Talented surgeons have detailed goals and a process to achieve them. The most talented surgeons have concrete goals, a process, and a timeline to achieve them, often with secondary goals waiting in the wings.

From a practical standpoint, the first step is to create short-term and long-term goals. Then you create a process to achieve those goals. For example, you want to finish the NYC marathon in under four hours—that defines your goal and may even be your personal record. The *process* is to then create a workout schedule for the four months prior to the race. The process may take into account an analysis that you are weak at running hills, so your training would then include hill repeat workouts. Adhere to the process, and make sure to celebrate the adherence to the process, not just the achievement. Surgical residents-in-training rarely make personal surgical goals despite wanting to achieve surgical excellence. They even more rarely create a process to achieve those goals.

It is important to differentiate dreams from goals. Dreams are where we want to end up. Goals are how we get there. I do an exercise with young surgeons who seek my advice to better their career. I ask "If there were no obstacles whatsoever, what is the vision of your ideal career and what kind of surgeon would you want to be?" Young sports specialists often express their dream job as being the physician for a professional team. While many dream, few formulate a plan to get there.

The best *product goals* should have a results-oriented feature to it that can be measured. As an example, your goal may be to reduce your complication rate with ACL surgery to one percent. *Process goals* are what it takes to get the product goals you set. Process goals often are neglected, but are emphasized by successful athletes. They have a "no excuses" attitude. They take full accountability.

A process goal for a runner may be to run four times this week and decrease the running pace by five seconds on each run. Creating an environment to enhance the process can reduce wavering. For example, check the weather the night before, select appropriate clothing for the weather, put out running shoes and gear beside your bed, go to sleep early. A process goal for a surgical resident may be to study the anatomy and technique for an ACL reconstruction and practice the surgery five times in the arthroscopy lab prior to the end of their rotation. A product goal would be to have achieved proficiency whereby an attending allows the surgical resident to perform an ACL reconstruction in its entirety as the primary surgeon.

I believe weaker surgeons fail to set goals and have no clear action plan. Intermediate skill surgeons have general goals. The most excellent surgeons have, at any given time, a set of goals and, along with it, a process to achieve the goals. The greatest closer in baseball history, Mariano Rivera, once said to me "I have seen some younger players who wish to become famous before they are good. They are concerned about recognition before their skill is developed. It used to be that you got good first . . . and then recognition followed."

Prioritize excellence by defining and executing your process goals.

8

Take chances outside of the operating room.

Often, surgeons execute aspects of a surgical procedure as it was taught to them without questioning the specific rationale or alternative options. Surgery, at the onset of training, encompasses a huge black box slowly opening. Diagnosis, indications for surgery, and surgical technique are learned and incorporated. More simply, you accept what you are taught with little question and apply it. Deviating from the instructed technique that results in poor surgery is not acceptable. Therefore, surgeons often prefer what is safe and reliable, but, in doing so, retard growth and true excellence.

While many surgeons perform surgery exactly the same way they were taught in residency, others evolve their skill and techniques commensurate with technology evolution. Seeking improvement can require exploring alternatives, and at times going out on the ledge or asking what may seem like silly questions. For example, when I was a fellow-in-training in 2001, a weekly conference was held to teach revision

ACL surgery. When revising a failed ligament surgery, the bone tunnel location for placing the new ACL graft is a critical factor for success. If the tunnel from the original surgery is in the correct position, the tunnel can be used again; when the tunnel is in an incorrect position, it cannot be used again. The technique to avoid an incorrect tunnel was an unsolved problem at that time.

I considered a solution and asked the group of senior surgeons a question on drilling the new tunnel in the femur bone—with a modification—starting from one of the routinely used skin incisions called the medial portal, which is customarily used to insert the arthroscopic instruments such as burs (like dental burs) into the knee joint. This offered a different trajectory for the tunnel and greater precision in the exact starting location. This would make it possible to create a tunnel in a proper position while avoiding the tunnel that was poorly placed. I was thinking, "problem solved." The senior surgeon's response condemned the idea saying, "It would risk violating the back wall and result in a 'blowout' or a tunnel that becomes structurally incompetent." This type of blowout complication was a major technical concern at the time.

I felt the response was reactionary, not analytical. I continued to probe the feasibility of my suggested solution despite stinging rejection. It was similar to falling down and having to get back up. Fast forward to today, surgeons now regularly drill from the medial portal revision

ACL surgery and also while performing primary ACL surgery. The techniques were refined and specialized instrumentation developed to make the technique an improvement of traditional techniques. The advantage is great precision in positioning an anatomic ACL. The closer the graft replicates normal anatomy, the better the graft will work, and the higher the success for the patient.

Surgery does not lend itself to swings and misses because of the obvious negative consequence to the patient. While physicians refer to the "practice of medicine," it is a far different practice than what is found in athletic practice. A surgeon, when performing an operation, does not have the equivalent of a driving range. Similarly, a major league pitcher would not try a new type of pitch in a critical playoff game. A surgeon's practice field is the surgical skills lab.

Reinhold Schmieding, President and Founder of Arthrex, Inc, a market-leading orthopaedic company, has enhanced the training of thousands of surgeons by providing them with the perfect surgeons' practice range—the surgical skills lab. In the lab, developing surgeons practice standard and complex surgical procedures on cadavers. Skill acquisition grows quickly in the lab after making inconsequential mistakes and correcting them. Surgeons also become aware of their surgical limitations as they take full advantage of the "reaching" component of skill development (reaching is discussed more in

Part 2). The best surgeons go to the lab often to instruct other surgeons—but what they are really doing is reaching and falling themselves as they try new techniques.

During practice sessions, Gretzky drilled maneuvers and fell down regularly because he pushes boundaries. Reaching and falling often makes you feel stupid. When it comes to developing talent however, mistakes are not really mistakes; they are guideposts you use to get better. This is really saying, "Take risks to reach further and use the stupid feeling to work even harder." Gretzky drilled by himself or with his teammates in practice and fell down. Game situations with true stakes do not provide the right environment to fall down. Creating opportunities to take chances is too often neglected.

During practice mode, take chances to refine your technique—don't wait until the big test.

9

Recognize the difference between hard skills and soft skills. All skills are either hard or soft. Hard skills arise from the ability to repeat tasks with precision—your golf swing, playing a solo on guitar, throwing a slider. They follow the **ABC** rule—**A**lways **B**e **C**onsistent— as pointed out by Dan Coyle in *The Little Book of Talent*. Soft skills are more improvisational and require decision-making based on available information—a soccer player sensing defensive weakness, or a businessperson reading a room while negotiating. They follow the 3 **R's**— **R**eading, **R**ecognizing, and **R**eacting. Hard and soft skills are very different, are developed differently, and use different parts of the brain.

Surgical skills are a complex balance of hard and soft skills. Hard skill examples include optimal patient positioning on the operating table, repeatable and precise prepping and draping, ideal portal creation for arthroscopy, and perfect tunnel placement for ligament surgery. Examples of soft skills include managing unexpected bleeding during the surgery, sudden recognition and management of unavailable instruments, quickly recognizing your assistant is inexperienced with the surgery.

Appreciate and differentiate hard and soft skills. You need both.

10

Master hard skills like Mariano Rivera.

Repeat with precision. It is like a sled on snow. The first track sets the second run. Go slow, perfect moves. Find errors and fix them. This is boring, but always saves time down the track. The basics of surgery require maddening attention to repetitive detail.

Mariano (Mo) Rivera's success is based on his ability to throw a single pitch with incredible accuracy and movement—"the cutter." Perfect wind up, perfect finger pressure applied to the ball, perfect timing of upper body motion while driving legs toward home plate, perfect ball release, and follow through. His precise linked steps of execution yield perfect location of the ball across the plate and with a late-breaking curve. Every hitter he faced, despite knowing the cutter was coming, found it to be unhittable.

Talented surgeons understand the critical importance of perfect patient positioning, perfect placement of the tourniquet, perfect draping, perfect positioning of the lighting, and perfect placement of the incision. These are the basics of surgery that, when mastered, provide excellent exposure. It then makes surgery look easy. Golfers seem to make everything look easy when everything is "set up perfectly." They practice and repeat with extraordinary precision. They execute their swing with different clubs and practice with the ball lying on different cuts of grass. They execute with perfect hand position, grip pressure, and lower and upper body coordination.

Positioning a patient imperfectly is like getting into your car with a seat that is too low and rearview and side mirrors that are poorly positioned, compromising your front, peripheral, and rear views. Imperfect draping further compromises your view, like having clutter on your dashboard. Imperfect placement of the incision is like having the steering wheel positioned too far away from you.

For a simple short drive, it can work, but if reaction to a child darting out into the street is instantly required—recognition and steering to avoid the child may be compromised, resulting in tragedy. Finally, poor tourniquet placement (tourniquets are used to minimize bleeding) will lead to bleeding that obscures the surgical field, which is like driving in the rain with broken wipers. Add a few imperfect driving conditions together with the other problems of seat in the wrong position, steering wheel too far away, mirrors poorly adjusted, dirty windows, dull windshield wipers and driving becomes appreciably more dangerous. The same is true for surgery.

Demand for hard skill perfection in the operating room should be the status quo—and, for anything else critically important in life.

11

Honor anatomy and enjoy surgical exposure—the hard skills of surgery.

Regardless of the discipline, manifesting any talent requires both hard and soft skills. For example, Tom Brady's ability to read a defense, select a receiver, and time the pass is a soft skill. Delivering an accurate pass is a hard skill. Hard skills are prioritized in early sports development. Technique is everything. Many talented athletes and musicians continue to drill the basics well into their careers and work on the same exercises they did when they were kids. Professional squash players get onto a court by themselves and practice 50 tight rail shots against the wall as they did when they picked up their very first squash racquet.

A saying exists—nothing changes a surgeon's behavior more than knowledge of anatomy. The fundamentals of surgery are based on comprehensive knowledge of anatomy. Most talented surgeons review anatomy on a regular basis much as an accomplished musician practices scales. Anatomy serves as a road map to creating surgical exposure, whereby the surgeon dissects and moves tissues to create a window to view the problem. The better the surgical exposure, the easier the surgery. Poor exposure is analogous to trying to fix a carburetor in a car with a hood that only opens partially. Talented surgeons always achieve great exposure and then make the surgery look elegant and easy.

The most feared complication of surgery is accidently cutting a nerve or vessel, with catastrophic consequence. Extreme knowledge of anatomy is the surgeon's protection. If you know where the nerves are, then you know where they aren't. Nerves aren't cut because of poor coordination; nerves are cut because of poor knowledge of anatomy and duress during the procedure, often because set-up and exposure is poor. The equivalent of a head coach saying "we beat ourselves tonight" is a surgeon who fails to get excellent exposure.

Honor the essential frame of your skill. In soccer, we honored ball handling skills. In cooking, honor the ingredient selection process—often thought of as more important than the execution. In music—honor scales.

There's no hard skill more important than mastering the basics—whether you're a surgeon reviewing anatomy, or a musician practicing scales.

12

To build soft skills, practice as if you are downhill skiing. Soft skills are beautiful. Behave aggressively, be curious, and experiment with new ways to challenge yourself. Consider the Brazilian lab of improvisation: futebal de salao (soccer in the room) or futsol. It's five-on-five on a basketball-sized field. Compared to a standard soccer game, a player may have 600 percent more touches on the ball in tight spaces while surrounded by other players. My college soccer career involved a tremendous amount of time dedicated to a game we call "5 vs. 2." This game is considered by many as the most effective return for time spent. Two defenders are inside a circle created by the other five players. The objective is for the five players to pass the ball to each other, often with only one touch to the ball allowed. The inside defenders have to chase and interrupt the passing. The defender then switches and becomes the attacker. This drill works well because the number of touches (or reaches) is extremely high and the pressure is high (tight space). The game can be

played with two balls. From the time a player receives the ball to when s/he passes it, the number of touches a player can make can be reduced from an unlimited number of times, to two touches, to one touch, further adding stress and higher intensity.

Most developing surgeons underestimate soft skills. Surgical talent is often referred to as having "good hands," the symbol of hard skill precision. Many believe that surgeons require steady hands like major league hitters need exceptional eyesight. In fact, it is rare for a Yankee position player to have vision that is less than 20-15. Surgeons, however, often display average hand coordination. Some of the most talented surgeons even have minor tremors during surgery. Finally, it is rare during the selection phase of new resident surgeons to assess any hand coordination aptitude.

So what are the soft skills that differentiate great surgeons from average ones? One explanation is that talented surgeons have superior decision-making skills under pressure (soft skills). Talented surgeons prioritize preparation for the surgery, respect complicated challenges, anticipate future problems, and avoid them. Talented surgeons somehow make routine cases look boringly easy and in extreme conditions respond without panic. Bobby More, a fabled legend English soccer player, was asked if he was "fast." His response was, "if you ask me to run from A to B and time me then I am slow. If you consider *when* I run from A to B then I am not so slow." Talented surgeons know when to extend the incision, know when to ask for an immediate transfusion of their patient, know when to accept good instead of great when catastrophe is looming.

In surgery, every experience, especially the misses or the near-mistakes, should be analyzed and maximized for growth. Surgeons need to practice like a skier going downhill who reacts instantly to unpredictable terrain and situations. They should create theoretical scenarios or surprises and then work out optimal solutions.

I conduct a weekly Surgical Technique Conference at Columbia University that is attended by residents, fellows, medical students and attending physicians. One such conference presented the surgical technique for elbow MCL reconstruction. During the explanation of bone tunnel creation, I asked developing residents what would be the next course of action if the bone bridge breaks. They typically say, "Use a different implant." I then ask, "Did you check if that implant was available before the surgery started?" The answer is frequently "No."

I then ask, "What do you do if your suggested replacement implant is not available?" Before you know it, they describe surgical maneuvers that create secondary problems such as catastrophic drilling through the ulnar nerve, causing permanent nerve damage. They fall down in the conference room and get more soft skill development than any smooth actual surgical experience in the operating room.

The Surgical Technique Conference is a method of scenario planning. Throughout the presentation, the questions asked are not "Why did you do that?" but rather "What would you do if . . . . ?" Josh Kaufman, in *The Personal MBA*, refers to this as counterfactual simulation. The "what if" part is counterfactual. It is a powerful tool to imagine what may occur in the future. Scenario planning is detailed and requires brain power. Often, young surgeons can't yet conceive what the possible scenarios are. With time, surgeons can do personal counterfactual simulation along with mental rehearsal and visualization as described in tips #25 and #35.

World-class performers don't use this feel-good approach either. They realize that they need to consider a mix of positive and negative outcomes to plan for the best process and achieve the best outcome. This "balanced positive approach" starts with considering the possible negative outcomes first to find and analyze weaknesses, insecurities and doubts. Then they visualize the positive, envisioning the best outcome, to put them in the right frame of mind.

Dan Coyle explained how this is used successfully by the U.S. Army Special Forces soldiers, the Green Berets. "Teams spend weeks training for a mission (most of which happen at night). On the day of the mission they follow a two-part routine. First, they spend the entire morning going over every possible mistake or disaster that could happen during the mission. Every possible screw up is mercilessly examined, and linked to an appropriate response: if the helicopter crash-lands, we'll do X. If we are dropped off at the wrong spot, we'll do Y. If we are outnumbered, we'll do Z. After some hours of doing this, the team takes a break and has lunch together. They socialize, relax, and maybe take a nap. Then they spend the afternoon in phase two, talking about everything going exactly right. They review each move, visualizing each step, and vividly imagine it going 100 percent perfectly."

What's important to remember with the Balanced-Positive Approach is that time is equally split: spending time first on the negative, and then on the positive. Many top performers take this approach (Peyton Manning, Steve Jobs are two). George St. Pierre is another. This former three-time Welterweight Champion of the Ultimate Fighting Championship has said this about his mental preparation, "I visualize fighting all the time . . . sometime[s] I'm getting beat. But I visualize how I'm going to turn that situation to my advantage."

Football teams also relentlessly plan scenarios and develop options. When their team is down by 14 points in the 4th quarter and within 30 yards of the end zone and it's 4th down with 1 yard to go—the coaching staff has already planned for it and has play options to choose from.

I often scenario plan surgery and even have trouble stopping. My mind runs like a computer and goes back to the beginning and runs another scenario again, like a loop or a skier who takes the lift up to the top and repeats the run slightly differently each time to challenge himself. The future is not easily predictable, but the more scenarios you have played out and prepared for, the better surgeon you will be.

Never stop asking "What if?"

———————

PART TWO:
IMPROVING SKILLS

**Deep training—Find the sweet
spot, then reach and repeat.**

*"There is a difference between people
in music and sports talent hotbeds and
ordinary people everywhere else—talented
people have a vastly different relationship
with practicing."*
—DAN COYLE, THE TALENT CODE

MANY CONSIDER PRACTICE to be painfully boring, unexciting, a grind. In hotbeds—practice *is* the game. In hotbeds, people hunt for *the sweet spot,* which is the zone where your ability is pushed just beyond your performance comfort. The process fundamentally requires **reaching**. An individual's velocity for acquiring skill (how fast he or she can gain mastery) is proportional to the amount of time spent practicing in the sweet spot. This is the critical explanation of why some learn a skill quickly and others simply fail to improve.

Early in school, math made physical sense to me and I enjoyed it. Recreationally, when I was not playing soccer (rainy days and evenings), I spent hours building model airplanes, rockets, and radio control cars. After I was accepted to Columbia University's School of Engineering and Applied Science, (Columbia was ranked in the top five soccer teams in the nation that year),

I explained to my parents that I wished to play soccer, study engineering, and then attend medical school. It didn't make sense to my father that engineering could properly prepare me for a career in medicine.

My goal was to practice sports medicine and surgery. Engineering's foundation is analytical thinking, developing a deep understanding of how things break or withstand stress. Sports medicine *is* the engineering of the body and its musculoskeletal system. I never fully convinced him that I was actually giving myself a competitive edge with engineering, but he went along with it. I use my engineering constantly as a surgeon, researcher, and thinker. And I have conceptualized the sweet spot, reaching, and learning velocity with simple mathematical equations.

"Strain" defined in engineering terms refers to stretching of a material and can be considered analogous to *reaching* for skill development. Mathematically, this is described as:

Strain = Change in Length of a Material / Original Length. (when a force is applied to the material)

Strain is often thought of as the stretch of a material when pulled apart.

The concept of experience is often misunderstood. In fact, patients seek and trust surgeons with tremendous experience. Experience in isolation does not equal better performance. Anyone who performs incorrectly—and happens to do it a lot—simply does it incorrectly and, unfortunately for patients if you're a surgeon, a lot. The typical commute to the hospital where I work is about 20 miles for most physicians, with some of the more senior surgeons having commuted for 30 years. Despite the repeated practice of driving to and from work, their driving ability has not changed at all. In fact, their driving safety may have declined with the introduction of cell phone use in the car.

Consider the equations:

TIME = EXPERIENCE

STRAIN × TIME = SKILL

Experience relates to time spent engaged in an activity. Skill relates to the amount of time multiplied by the effort or strain. Most people who drive home from work are not straining to improve their driving. Years go by and no improvement is observed in their driving. Surgeons and all professionals can fall into the same trap—as years pass, they may never realize their lack of development because they're not straining or stretching themselves.

The quality of anyone's practice can be equated to the amount of effort and how specific the activity is to the desired skill. Quality of practice is overwhelmingly more important than the amount of time spent. The 10,000-hour rule to become an expert was highlighted by Malcolm Gladwell in *Outliers.* However, focused practice, with continuous reaches, feedback, and correction, is more important than the amount of time spent.

Residents sense the most gratification during their surgical training when they operate as the primary surgeon. As the primary surgeon, the resident is doing the physical technical aspects and making decisions as the surgery progresses. It is similar to going to a sports camp where the best part of camp is the games played at the end of the day. Surgeons experience and enjoy the thrill of operating just as athletes enjoy competition. It is true that operating is thrilling; at times, it can be compared to surfers who wait and wait for a brief six-second ride on a wave. Many residents, therefore, choose training programs where the operating experience is known to be high. They often misunderstand, however, how operating experience, if done in a leisurely, enjoyable way, fails to develop actual surgical skill development.

I developed an early reputation during my training for surgical skill. Yet, my resident case volume—the amount of physical surgery I performed or assisted on while in training—I estimate to be in the bottom 10 percent of all surgeons during that training period. How can surgery be mastered then? Is this the prodigy myth? The answer is in the equation. I believe

I reached further than other surgeons, and at every opportunity I maximized the effort made, focused my practice, solicited and responded to feedback to overcome the limited time spent. Appreciating the power of the effort or reaching component to the skill equation, my skill grew at an aggressive rate.

I made surgical practice the game: true through today, leisure operating does not occur in my operating room.

13

Capitalize on the compounding effect of skill acquisition. Albert Einstein called *compounding interest* "the greatest mathematical discovery of all time." My retirement plan, like many of my friends', includes investments in diversified funds and some ETFs (exchange-traded funds). Initially, growth of the principal was slow and the plotted curve of the amount of money versus time spent was flat. But, as time passed, the growth curve began to steepen slowly and then sharply, and the compounding effect became profound. The wonder of compounding requires two things: the re-investment of earnings and time. The more time you give your investments, the more you are able to accelerate the income potential of your original investment, which exponentially separates you from the rest of the pack.

Compounding is an example of a feedback loop where the output of the system becomes one of the inputs for the next cycle. Positive reinforcing loops amplify the system's output with each system cycle. Reinforcing loops can lead to blockbusting growth within a short time. Compounding can be applied to everyday life and can be capitalized on in skill development. For example, the earliest phase of surgical training includes participating in small, uncomplicated surgical procedures. Graduated responsibility ensues and, as more skills are mastered, those skills are reinvested in a way that more advanced surgical opportunities are presented to the developing surgeon.

The forward-motion cycle moves quickly for some surgeons who engage in effort-filled deep practice. The better you are early on, the more operating responsibilities you are given and, in turn, the better you get with more of these practice opportunities (feed forward loop). In addition, the better you are—in skill and knowledge—the more learning you derive from each surgery. Many find the skill advancement to be fulfilling thereby fueling deeper, effortful practice, creating a beautiful and viscous cycle for growth. If you are at the beginning of your curve and feel you are not starting the growth aspect of your curve, put in more time and more concentrated effort. Accelerated growth is just around the corner.

Does compounding occur in sports? Youth hockey players who show early skill development are placed with better players to increase their challenge. They even get superior coaching as they continue to excel. This gets them into a compounding environment. This is true of any endeavor: soccer, chess, math class, you name it.

Recently, I reviewed my personal compounding. My first investment was during medical school, in anatomy class. I spent many hours beyond what was required dissecting the extremities of cadavers simply because I liked and got "hooked" as I got better at it. The course work required dissecting the elbow, forearm and hand on the cadaver. After completion I did it again on the opposite side. I then dissected all the unfinished dissections on my classmates' cadavers. I developed my skill with surgical instruments late at night, alone, in the cadaver lab.

As my second investment, I dedicated a full year to orthopaedic research. During that time, I performed experiments on cadaver knees which required accurate dissection followed by actual surgical procedures. Later, when I began operating with attending physicians as a "new intern surgeon," they gave me quick advancements in operating opportunities.

In my third year of surgical training, I was assigned to help an attending surgeon with knee arthroscopy cases that required a more senior-level surgeon because the attending lacked confidence in those procedures. (There are a very few experienced attending surgeons who still benefit from the help of a solid resident to get a good result.) With that established confidence, I was able to convince a trauma and knee specialist to perform arthroscopy when he typically would not consider it. As an example, knee fractures affecting the upper shin bone (called tibial plateau fractures) often have associated injury to the knee shock absorber cartilage tissue (called meniscus). The meniscal damage associated with the fracture was often simply neglected because the more major injury of the tibial plateau fracture takes priority. I argued convincingly to the senior attending that the meniscus could arthroscopically be repaired in combination with the tibial plateau fracture surgery. Soon, I had more experience in fixing menisci than chief residents two years ahead of my training. I then worked with a general orthopaedic surgeon who ran two rooms simultaneously. One room was typically an arthroscopy room that required a senior resident because of the technical nature of the complex procedures. I ran that room and did all the arthroscopies that rotation. (That same surgeon, four years later, asked me if I would perform arthroscopy on his knee that had a meniscus tear. The biggest compliment for a young attending is for your former teacher to request you as his surgeon.)

Put in focused and effort-filled practice early in your career/training to experience the compounding effect. Start the compounding today.

54

14

Practice alone as if you were preparing for a musical performance. Solo

practice works, but many avoid it. Solo practice is the best way to: 1) seek out the edge of your ability (your sweet spot), and 2) develop consistent discipline because it doesn't depend on others. A classic study of musicians compared world-class performers with top amateurs. The research found that the two groups were similar in every practice variable except one: world-class performers spent five times as many hours practicing *alone*.

Not all disciplines lend themselves to solo practice. For example, how do you practice surgery on your own? Read, take notes on instructional videos of surgery and then rehearse surgery again and again. Consider surgery a performance: like a theatrical rendition of the Lion King on Broadway or playing a Beatles song on guitar. If you were challenged to perform a song to a large audience at the end of the month, it would make clear sense to practice alone without distraction as much as possible.

Talented surgeons practice procedures in the lab on their own. Some of the most advanced surgical residents are those who work constantly in the lab. I recall doing extensive dissections in the anatomy lab beyond what any others were doing, learning to handle soft tissue, and understanding anatomical relationships.

Practicing alone also gives you the autonomy to decide what is most important to practice. In many ways, it is important to eliminate/reduce your largest weakness and balance that with what you may consider to be most important. The best way to learn anatomy is with solo practice. Study from a book, quiz yourself, and then engage in cadaver dissections. I recently instructed a surgical skills lab teaching developing surgeons. One of our most promising residents in attendance chose to work alone on her cadaver instead of breaking for lunch. I expect her to excel throughout her career. As the North Carolina University women's soccer coach Anson Dorrance said, "The vision of a champion is someone who is bent over, drenched in sweat, at the point of exhaustion, when no one else is watching."

I, too, am always looking for that champion resident who has been up all night and still pressing, bent over tirelessly working on his or her skill, when no one is watching.

15

Obsess over the fundamental details like Coach Wooden.

During my own training, I was initially shocked to see how often surgeons have tremendous difficulty during routine elective surgery. I had a prejudice that, because surgery was so impactful to patients, and surgeons were so well selected and trained, routine surgery would happen with a predictably spectacular performance every time. In contrast, my experience was more like seeing a hitter in the middle of the season who is zero for 20 and loses all confidence at the plate. As I was exposed to a large number of surgeons, it became clear to me that they could be categorized in one of the following categories:

1) makes it look easy, whose product is excellent;
2) makes it look easy, but the product is poor (they take shortcuts);
3) makes it look hard (they struggle), but the product is good;
4) makes it look hard and the product is poor.

Surgeons become creatures of habit; the best ones put effort into making excellence a habit. Like all disciplines, effective surgery requires extreme attention to detail. I use patient positioning and draping as an isolated component of surgery to emphasize the power of attention to detail.

Therefore, residents on their very first day of working with me go through draping instruction, the doldrums of their first day. For example, for elbow arthroscopy, the patient must be positioned with the elbow flexed and elevated above shoulder level. The patient's bean bag support must be away from his chest so it does not compete with the arthroscopy instruments. Before accepting the patient position and beginning surgery, mime the surgery with pretend instruments and test the set-up for flaws. If not correct or if it's less than perfect, adjust it.

The next step is draping. Surgery is done under sterile conditions. We wash hands and use expensive sheets that are sterile to isolate the surgical field. Yet, a cavalier attitude develops amongst the team and draping becomes contaminated or touched with non-sterile objects or people regularly. Our immediate concern is risk of surgical infection but, for me, it is not that infection risk is going to dramatically rise, it's the deviation from perfection on small details that arrests development as an elite surgeon. In addition, since it is the start of the case, any problems here profoundly affect everything that happens later in the case.

I obsess over perfect surgical draping. Coach John Wooden obsessed over perfect donning of socks. Coach John Wooden has won 10 NCAA basketball championships at UCLA; he won 88 straight games and executed four perfect seasons earning enormous recognition and a platform for others to research excellence. His approach to detail, as it turns out, is strikingly similar to surgery. Wooden, on the first day of practice at the start of a season, would sit his team down and teach them how to put on their shoes and socks. Yes, put on their shoes and socks.

"You know, basketball is a game that's played on a hardwood floor," Wooden has been quoted as saying. "And to be good, you have to change your direction, and change your pace. That's hard on your feet. Your feet are very important. And if you don't have every wrinkle out of your sock . . . Now put it in wide, now pull it up . . . Now, don't grab these lines up here, go down, eyelet by eyelet . . . each one, that's it. Now, pull it in there . . . Tie it like this . . . There's always a danger of becoming untied when you are playing," he said. "If they become untied, I may have to take you out of the game . . . in practice, I will have to take you out. Miss practice and you're going to miss playing time and, not only that, it will irritate me a little, too."

Little things make big things happen. Everything in surgery is connected. All details are connected to other details as part of a whole. I have observed draping several thousand times by several hundred surgeons and even older, senior surgeons. I am at a point where I could assess a lot on the single fundamental of draping alone.

Some people obsess over what other people think, some of what the weather will be like, some with the bonus they expect at the end of the quarter. I obsess over the details of surgery.

16

Mime it and mimic it. Developing surgeons should do everything possible to mimic the moves of the expert surgeon. With time, they improve; technique becomes automatic and similar to the experts. Then, with more time, they shape it into their own style. During arthroscopic procedures, the surgery is performed with a camera inside the joint and the procedure may be viewed on the screen. Most people in the room end up watching the screen. The resident who watches the hand movements will learn more and can then even mime the hand movements. Where is the index finger; is the instrument held like a pencil or like a golf club? Sometimes the instrument is held upside down.

When I was a fellow, I practiced MCL reconstructive surgery in the lab, following my mentors with exactness for positioning and exposure. At talent hotbeds, you will see people swinging golf clubs and tennis rackets at empty air, playing the piano on tabletops, and skiing imaginary slalom courses with their feet fixed on the floor.

It looks crazy, but from a deep-practice perspective, it makes sense. Removing everything except the essential action lets you focus on what matters most: making the right reach. I am currently taking guitar lessons from a Julliard musician. While he shows me chord progressions with complicated finger positions on the board, I literally play air guitar attempting to replicate him. I know shortly he is going to ask me to give the section a try.

If you are watching a master surgeon in the OR, or a Food Network cooking show on how to professionally cut an onion, free your hands and start mimicking their movements.

17

Isolate the sweet spot. You reach the sweet spot when you put yourself at the edge of your ability, which is where you learn the best and quickest. Talented people always find it. Your comfort zone is where things are easy and effortless; you'll succeed 80 percent or more of the time here. The sweet spot is difficult, elicits frustration, creates alertness to errors, forces a struggle, and requires full engagement. The percentage of successful attempts approximates 50-80 percent. If you push even further, you will arrive at the survival zone, which evokes confusion, desperation, guessing, and a feeling of being overmatched. Your success rate will be less than 50 percent. The test of the sweet spot is: if you absolutely tried your hardest, what could you almost accomplish?

New surgical residents and medical students almost always begin their surgical skill training tying knots for sutures. It comes pretty quickly. Then, most think the skill is mastered. But knot tying in the operating room is different. You need to practice wearing two layers of surgical gloves, which changes your tactile sense. You practice deep in a hole. Tie the suture around something delicate: a small vessel that, if pulled, will break. Tie knots away from your body. Practicing golf with your ball lying perfectly in the fairway does not prepare you for an actual golf match where your ball can lie in ruts, uneven grass, or on the side of a hill.

Push to find your sweet spot with every aspect of any skill you wish to improve upon.

18

Engage deeply and embrace the struggle.

At all the talent hotbeds, the same facial expressions are observed: eyes narrow, jaw tight, nostrils flared. It's the face of someone intently reaching for something, falling short, and reaching again. Full engagement requires complete focus with a "kill-to-get-it-right" approach. Almost all talented athletes, musicians, and chess players agree that effortful practice is mentally exhausting.

For example, I have become quite adept at using GPS. I travel from Westport, CT, to Yankee Stadium and use a GPS while listening to sports radio or an audio book. The travel is interrupted with "Prepare to exit right in one mile onto 87 South." One day, the GPS was not working. I quickly realized how helpless I was in getting to the stadium despite having repeated the drive many times. This is an example of repetition with no effort.

Residents often want to be the driver during surgery, but are without knowledge of the destination. They are learning how to steer the car, apply the brakes, and put on the windshield wipers, but if the attending physician is not there, they have no idea where to go.

If you are a passenger in a car, you may feel as if you are not gaining skill as a driver. If you are the passenger in the car and giving directions, perhaps, you are getting better by looking at the different routes, studying the traffic, putting on the radio. You are doing so many things, but not steering the wheel. Residents want to steer the wheel. But to get there, which is most important for a patient's successful outcome, it's critical to study and know the routes.

During surgery, residents may have been in the OR from 7 a.m. to 10 p.m. and may have had the metaphorical GPS on the entire time.

Most of us who practice do not recognize that the necessary level of engagement required for deep practice is not measured in the number of minutes or hours, but in the number of high-quality reaches and repetitions you make. Don't consider time, but rather high-quality repetitions. Most talented people think that what limits their training is being unable to push through the mental strain.

In *Talent is Overrated,* Geoff Colvin discussed Nathan Milstein, one of the 20th century's greatest violinists, who was a student of the famous teacher Leopold Auer. Milstein asked Auer if he practiced enough. Auer responded, "Practice with your fingers and you need all day. Practice with your mind and you will do as much in one and a half hours."

The course to excellence is really the road less travelled. As Matthew Syed stated in *Bounce*, "Think of life as having two paths: one leading to mediocrity, the other to excellence. What do we know about the path to mediocrity? Well, we know it is flat and straight. We know that it is possible to cruise along on autopilot with a nice, smooth, steady, almost effortless progression. We know above all, that you can reach the destination without stumbling or falling over.

"The path to excellence could not be more different. It is steep, grueling, and arduous. It is inordinately lengthy, requiring a minimum of 10,000 hours of lung-busting effort to get to the summit. And, most important of all, it forces voyagers to stumble and fall on every single stretch of the journey."

Insanity has been defined by Albert Einstein as doing the same thing over and over again and expecting a different outcome. Deep practice feels like an insane struggle. Most of us avoid struggle because it is mentally painful, with a feeling of failure that connects to your inner core. But, struggle is the biologic ingredient for skill to blossom. You need to seek out the frustration you feel at the edge of your ability. Your brain works like your muscles: no pain, no gain.

I remember sitting on a stool at age 12 with my guitar instructor demonstrating to me a classical piece. I never listened to classical music.

I squinted and focused as hard as I could. I watched his finger patterns on the fret board and repeated them on mine. We started back at the beginning with each mistake. I was exhausted after 10 minutes of working on it. My internal dialogue was, "I will get this and nothing, absolutely nothing, will stop me from getting this." Then suddenly I was getting it and it drove me even harder to keep it going. My teacher said to me, "I have never had a student learn that fast!" Right then, I recognized the power of intense deep practice. If it's not uncomfortable, it's not working. Embracing the struggle with a mental attitude of "I will get this" is essential.

Where does the motivation come from to engage in struggle? We intuitively think the willingness to embrace the struggle originates from deep inside us. Psychologist Carol Dweck and others argue otherwise. Motivation is largely social; fueled by our interactions with the people around us. In other words, motivation is less about what's in your heart, and more about how you connect with your social circle.

Get comfortable with the uncomfortable.

19

Believe you are better than your mentor.

Surgical training follows an apprenticeship model where an intern works with a "master." During this process, I stumbled across a technique to enhance deep engagement (tip #18). I found myself silently challenging my attending master surgeon. Why isn't he doing the surgery better? I asked myself, "Why isn't he just passing the suture through the bone tendon junction to achieve the fastest suture passing and strongest suture fixation?"

Believing or pretending that you are actually better than the master is a method to force an increase in the intensity of your practice. To embrace the struggle, I began every surgery I assisted in with the belief that I could perform the surgery better than the master attending. With every move the attending made, I painstakingly mentally explored other options for better exposure, better fixation, better efficiency of movements, better instruments, even better relationships with the surgical team. I would have an incredible internal dialogue with myself as I kept up with every move during the surgery.

This takes passivity out of the assistant and replaces it with incredible mental strain. Because it is not fun—like sports drills. It's like the many young basketball players who simply want to play and do not want to do lay-up drills. Most people won't do it, but some will embrace the challenge to be better than the master.

I would watch surgeries and predict how poor moves would propagate difficulty later in the case. While the difficulty was frustrating to the attending surgeon, I felt satisfaction in "knowing and developing a deeper understanding" of what was creating the chaos. I applied these mental games to every surgery I assisted with. I had intense internal brain chatter about the surgery that pressed my mental involvement. Surgeons in training who are slow to develop talent are those who passively hold a retractor after the surgeon properly positions it. The execution of questioning every surgical step and the consequence of all options should be both taxing and draining—consistent with the growth theories previously presented. While I created a mental framework where I pretended I was better than the attending surgeon as an exercise tool, I always maintained a respect for their position and the decisions they were making.

Another way to engage is to pretend that you will only see the operation demonstrated to you once, and only once, before you have to perform it yourself. You have to take full advantage of that one opportunity so you can do it the next time by yourself.

Critically observe your mentor's process, and look for ways to improve it.

20

Break surgery down into pieces. I have noticed that some people seem to be good at everything; I mean everything. They win in billiards, they win at table tennis, they win at golf, they catch the most on the river when fly-fishing, they win at the board game Risk, they win at Scrabble, they play violin, they cook, and make custom furniture for their house. These people seek out new things to try. I often believe they develop proficiency in so many things because of their mental make-up. If they get the itch, they will devote themselves to it until they get it. These are among the few people I know who can actually assemble furniture from IKEA. I have come to learn that these oh-so-few who are good at oh-so-many things succeed because of their approach. It's a simple approach that is described in Josh Kaufman's book *The First 20 Hours: How to Learn Anything . . . Fast*. Kaufman explains that rapid skill acquisition requires four steps: 1) Deconstructing the skill into the smallest possible sub-skills; 2) Learning each sub-skill;

3) Removing physical, mental, and emotional barriers that obstruct practice; 4) Practice the most important sub-skills.

What is the single smallest element of any skill I can master? What other elements link to that element? No matter what skill you set out to learn, the pattern is always the same. See the whole thing. Break it down to its simplest elements. Put it back together. Repeat. Practice one element and master it, then connect the next element. For example, a musician may break a piece into sections, such as the beginning, middle, and end of the song and learn each section independent of the other section. The individual sections are then mastered and subsequently combined for a final result. Chess is taught in sections of the opening, the middle game, and the end game.

Surgery is all about specific elements. Each procedure has: 1) Patient positioning 2) Surgical exposure 3) Pathology correction 4) Closure of the dissected tissues and wound.

The best surgeons, like the best chefs or chess players, break it down, master it, and reassemble the pieces.

21

Slow it down. When we learn how to do something new, we often want to rush to the end of the task. This urge for speed makes perfect sense, but it can also create sloppiness, particularly when it comes to hard skills. We trade precision, and long-term performance, for temporary thrill. So, slow it down.

Super-slow practice works like a magnifying glass: It lets us sense our errors more clearly, and this fixes them. Slow practice is used by many talent hotbeds to teach hard skills, from the Spartak Tennis Club (where students swing in such slow motion they resemble ballet dancers) to the Septien School of Contemporary Music (where performers learn a new song by singing one slow note at a time). Ben Hogan, considered to have perhaps the most technically sound golf swing in the history of the game, routinely practiced so slowly that when he finally contacted the ball, it moved about an inch. As the saying goes, "It's not how fast you can do it; it's how slowly you can do it correctly."

Each surgical procedure has greater critical aspects to it, where mistakes during that time period can have tremendous consequences, and other parts of the surgery can have blunders that have little or no effect on the patient. In the same way, Navy fighter pilots understand that take off and landing from an aircraft carrier are the most critical to a flight. Great surgeons know when to slow it down during a surgery and eliminate distractions.

Perfect your skill in slow motion first.

_____

22

When you get it right, mark the spot.

One of the most fulfilling moments of a practice session is when you have your first perfect repetition. When this happens, freeze. Rewind the mental tape and play the move again in your mind. Memorize the feeling, the rhythm, the physical and mental sensation. The point is to mark this moment—this is the spot where you want to return again and again. This is not the finish—it's the new starting line for perfecting the skill until it becomes automatic. As Kimberly Meier Sims of the Sato Center for Suzuki Studies says, "Practice *begins* when you get it right."

I often schedule the similar surgical procedures consecutively. The purpose is to make the surgical team work well and efficiently after the first case. The surgeon also has the opportunity to memorize the feel of doing it perfectly. Starting with the simplest case and progressing to more complex cases builds confidence. Every case has a beginning, middle, and end. Many aspects of complicated cases reproduce parts of simpler cases. The strategy to get it right and then repeat includes doing the simple surgeries first, getting it right, then repeating in subsequent surgeries that day. If an aspect of the surgery goes perfectly, the surgeon can "lock it in" by writing it down and then repeat with the subsequent surgery to further cement it.

Once you get it right, before you celebrate, do it correctly five more times.

23

Try a smaller incision. Smaller practice spaces can deepen practice when they are used to increase the number and intensity of the reps. A good example is used by FC Barcelona, widely considered one of the world's best soccer teams. The method is simple: you need one room slightly bigger than a bathroom, two players, and one ball. Whoever can keep the ball from the other player the longest wins. The little game isolates and compresses a vital skill—ball control—by creating a series of urgent, struggle-filled crises to which the players respond and thus improve.

Dan Coyle also describes the application of this outside of physical space. Poets and writers shrink the field by using restrictive meters to force themselves into a small creative form—such as haiku and micro-writing exercises. Comedy writers use the 140-character arena of Twitter as a space to hone their skills. Businesses can also benefit from compression: Toyota trains new employees by shrinking the assembly line to a single room filled with toy-sized replicas of its equipment. The company has found that this mini-training is more effective than training on the actual production line.

Ask yourself: what's the minimum space needed to make these reaches and reps? Where is extra space hindering fast and easy communication?

In surgery, we often outline the ideal incision and then shorten the incision. Why? The thinking is it is less morbid for the patient, or the patient will be more satisfied with a smaller scar. The unspoken element is that this applies additional pressure to the surgeon. Make the competition greater, make the situation even more challenging, make it more focused. A smaller incision requires greater depth of concentration and technical skill with manipulation of the tissues. It also raises the risk for a mistake. In orthopaedic surgery, "minimally invasive" surgery has become a marketing tool and numerous research studies have demonstrated an initial, higher complication rate with minimally invasive surgery. The complications are likely a product of working in the sweet spot. Avoid patient complications, but to improve, progressively shrink your incision.

Masters will find new ways to challenge their skill. Find your way to challenge yourself.

24

To learn from a book, close the book.

Like any serious profession, surgery is a lifelong process of education. Information has exploded and effective learning is a critical piece to achieving mastery. Dan Coyle has described a new concept in memorization. He describes a scenario where you pretend that in one week you will take a test on 10 pages of a book and you have 30 minutes to study. Which practice would help you get a better grade?

A) Reading those 10 pages four times in a row and trying to memorize them.

B) Reading those 10 pages once, then closing the book and writing a one-page summary.

It's not even close. Research shows that people who follow strategy B remember 50 percent more material over the long term than people who follow strategy A. This is due to one of the most fundamental rules of any deep practice: Learning is reaching. Passively reading a book—a relatively effortless process; letting the words wash over you like a warm bath—doesn't put you in the sweet spot. Less reaching equals less learning.

On the other hand, closing the book and writing a summary forces you to figure out the key points (one set of reaches), process and organize those ideas so they make sense (more reaches), and write them on the page (still more reaches, along with repetition). The equation is always the same: more reaching equals more learning.

Many surgeons believe they can get through a procedure by reading about it and then trying it on a patient. It is better to read about it, then write the case down on paper recounting the step-by-step details. Even better is when you get done writing each step in detail, crumple the paper up, and do it again. The mental rehearsal forces you to understand what aspects of the surgery you don't understand. This requires extreme mental labor to visualize the surgery from beginning to end and can be extremely powerful.

Surgeons need to develop objective metrics to work on their performance. As an example, you can prepare for surgery by reading the surgical technique the night before the surgery or you can attempt to write down the surgery step-by-step the night before the surgery, then compare this to the written textbook description, and then adjust how you study. Do it again until you get it perfect. Then do it again and question why each step is done in the sequence it is done and probe the reasons.

Read the book or watch the movie. Then stop and write a summary. It's the best way to learn.

25

Write the operative report before you perform every surgery.

The greatest displays of surgery are created twice. First they are created in the mind; then they are created in the operating room. Every surgical procedure requires a legal narrative of the surgery explaining the indications, findings during the operation, and details of the surgery performed. The operative report is part of the patient's legal medical record. Writing the operative report prior to the surgery is an exercise that forces step-by-step surgical planning. It requires rehearsing the surgery and helps avoid tragic mistakes. Complex surgery, such as a multiple knee ligament reconstruction, may require writing it down several times prior to the actual surgery.

As Tom Coughlin, the head coach of the New York Giants, has preached, earning the right to win through extreme preparation is analogous to earning the right to have a successful surgical performance. "If you wanted to execute anything better, prior to it, you could write down your steps and then analyze it."

Whatever your next contest, practice, or challenge is—write down your plan of execution and expected result before the engagement.

———————

26

Practice immediately after performance.

This tip is about the freshness that comes in the moment just after a performance, game, or competition. At that moment, practicing is probably the last thing you want to do. But it's the first thing you should do if you're not too worn out because it helps you target your weak points and fix them. As the golfer Jack Nicklaus said, "I always achieve my most productive practice after an actual round. Then the mistakes are fresh in my mind and I can go to the practice tee and work specifically on those mistakes."

After surgery, or another aspect of patient care, I usually to go into a room alone and review the events with conscious thought on how to improve. The process is a critique of what could be improved, but also includes how it will actually be improved for the next case. As an example, if I have difficulty passing the graft, the next time, the graft is conditioned and sized. I never make that mistake again. Forming solutions is better than simply acknowledging problems. Work on creating a solution. Reflect on surgery immediately afterwards.

Discuss the case with friends. Review your notes, find where you deviated. Most importantly, decide what went wrong and why. Then commit to never letting it happen again.

I recently struggled while fixing a broken bone located in the back of the elbow called the olecranon. This olecranon was badly displaced and broken in several pieces. During the operation, the fracture was being fixed with screws and a plate. When a fluoroscopy machine was used to analyze the quality of the reduction and screw placement, we discovered that the fracture had moved out of position. I made the decision to redo everything. I had to take the plate and screws out and start again. The final reduction and fixation was very acceptable and, in fact, quite good, but the need to redo it was a learning opportunity. Following the surgery, I met with the fellow to review the case and we studied it together. We came up with five improvements and options that could be implemented easily. One week later, I treated a similar fracture with the improvement plan. Had I not worked on those improvements after the surgery, I would not have been able to come up with them later.

Practice after performance until you come up with five things that can improve your next performance.

27

Practice using the R.E.P.S. technique.

Dan Coyle describes a simple technique used for skill development that employs the already described tips and creates a practice strategy to maximize effectiveness. It's a practical recipe called R.E.P.S. Each letter stands for a key element of deep practice:

R—Reach

E—Engagement

P—Purposefulness

S—Strong, speedy feedback

Let's define each of them.

Element 1: REACHING AND REPEATING. Does the practice have you operating on the edge of your ability, reaching, and repeating?

This is how to find the sweet spot. Make sure you are always in the sweet spot when you practice.

Element 2: ENGAGEMENT. Is practice immersive? Does it use emotion to propel you toward a goal?

This is the summation of tips on engagement, embracing the struggle, and pretending or striving to be better than the master. Get the most intensity out of any situation or training environment.

Element 3: PURPOSEFULNESS. Does the task directly connect to the skill you want to build?

Use self-reflection to determine what areas are most in need of improvement and what areas are most critical to performance. As an example, if you are a highly skilled soccer player, but your conditioning is poor, you will fail to perform well in the second half of games and will be unable to practice with duration and intensity. It then makes the most sense to work on conditioning that will enhance skill development

Element 4: STRONG, SPEEDY FEEDBACK. Does the learner receive a stream of accurate information about his or her performance— where s/he succeeded and where s/he made a mistake?

When a hitter makes an out and walks into the dugout and disappears into a tunnel, he is not going to get a drink or change his shoes. He is going to a video room to review his last swing.

Seek immediate feedback. Surgeons can self-reflect and surgeons in training can seek feedback from attendings immediately after surgical performance. You need feedback that is constantly available. Lack of feedback is like a chef trying to improve who does not ever taste her food, like a golfer hitting over a hill who can't track his ball flight, or like a musician wearing ear plugs.

The idea of this gauge is simple: When given a choice between two practice methods, or when you're inventing a new test or game, pick the one that maximizes the four qualities, the ones with the most R. E. P. S. The larger lesson here is to pay attention to the design of your practice. Small changes in method can create large increases in learning velocity.

"The key question to keep asking is, Are you spending your time on the right things? Because time is all you have."

—RANDY PAUSCH, THE LAST LECTURE

PART THREE:
ACHIEVING MASTERY

Develop motivation, grit, and analytical honesty

THE KREBS CYCLE is the chemical reaction by which aerobic organisms generate energy. It is very complicated. Every surgeon was required to learn it in college and in medical school as part of mandatory biology course work. Mastering understanding of the Krebs cycle requires an immense amount of work. Most students study hard, and then proudly declare they have nailed it. Years later, these same students-turned-surgeons fail to attach the same importance to appreciating the essential foundation of anatomy, or gaining familiarity, with the steps of surgery when training and preparing for a surgical procedure. There is often an expectation that attending surgeons will walk them through the surgery leisurely, like having a chauffeur taking them from home to work.

The surgeon's responsibility is to give the patient his or her best and should demand an effort 100-times greater than the effort put in to the study of the Krebs cycle. I often question why surgeons put much more effort into mastering the Krebs cycle as students than they currently do in preparing to provide optimal patient care with their surgical skill.

I believe surgeons face a supreme test every day while on the job. Patients entrust them to perform surgery with the confidence they will do an outstanding procedure. I instill in residents that, if they studied harder for the Krebs cycle test than they did for the surgery they are going to assist, they already have failed. Young surgeons must understand that the tests they took and the systems they developed to acquire knowledge, now must be applied at their most extreme level for surgery preparation and surgical knowledge and skill development. Paradoxically, this is when some residents seem to shut it off. Perhaps it is because life prior to this was all about getting the high grade. A culture shaped by many years of schooling and surgical training has to instill the new supreme goal and test, which is to provide the best care possible to people who trust them.

The motivation to master the Krebs cycle may be explained by theories of extrinsic motivation. Extrinsic motivation refers to the performance of an activity to attain an outcome. Common extrinsic motivations are rewards (e.g., money or grades) for demonstrating the desired behavior, and punishment following misbehavior. Competition is an extrinsic motivator because it encourages the performer to win and to beat others, not simply to enjoy the intrinsic rewards of the activity. A cheering crowd and the desire to win a trophy are also extrinsic incentives.

Treating patients and improving their quality

of life should be motivated by a different engine. Social psychology research suggests extrinsic rewards can lead to a subsequent reduction in intrinsic motivation. In one study, children who were rewarded with a ribbon and a gold star for drawing pictures spent less time playing with the drawing materials in subsequent observations than children who were assigned to an unexpected reward condition.

28

Grade your surgery. I give myself a letter grade for the completion of every surgical procedure and share it with my residents and fellows. Often, the grade is harsh. The intent is to foster self-critique. Talent hotbeds are full of little tests. The tests aren't scientific, and they are not treated as verdicts—they're far more like targeted workouts, invented by the performers and their teachers. For example, Tiger Woods created a test in which he has to hit a certain percentage of shots inside a certain distance each day (80 percent of eight irons within 20 feet, for example). I often grade each individual component of surgery to further break down the analysis. I take notes on the areas that need improvement and reflect on them on a regular basis. In preparation for another surgery, I make a forceful plan not to repeat the same mistakes.

What grade did you last get? And what did you do about it?

_____

29

Let go of ego. Surgery creates psychological conflict where it is egodystonic (in conflict with a
person's ideal self-image) to acknowledge that
you may have compromised another human's
body and future. The inability to be self-critical is
perhaps the most common roadblock to improvement that I see in mid-level-skill surgeons. The
ability to shift from ignoring mistakes to capital-
izing on mistakes may be the largest separating
characteristic of weak performers or surgeons
compared to the more elite.

I, personally, exaggerate the process of self-
critique because of its power. Self-critique may
be considered a skill to build skills. Self-critique
takes practice and needs to be done mindfully.
I take time to write down notes on good and bad
areas of surgical cases and how I felt about the
performance, whether it was surgical or how
I delivered a diagnosis to a concerned elite player
or the worried parent of a young child. I seldom
receive "A"s.

Top surgeons always see outside themselves,
a quality that has been referred to as "meta

cognition" or the ability to self-observe. Top performers are always more critical and more specific in their criticism of themselves. Top performers never blame others or circumstances for poor performance. Average surgeons, for example, believe poor results are out of their control. They blame the equipment, anesthesia team, or residents. Top surgeons are like top golfers who take personal responsibility and never blame the wind conditions.

Why do surgeons fail to give themselves honest feedback? The answer may be in the theory of cognitive dissonance. Cognitive dissonance is the distressing mental state that people feel when strong expectations do not meet reality, creating feelings of uneasiness, or dissonance. The dissonance of believing you are a good surgeon who would not harm a patient when you actually made a mistake that results in harm certainly challenges the individual surgeon's psyche.

The Greek poet Aesop introduced a fitting fable that describes a fox strolling along on a hot summer day when he came upon a vineyard. The fox crept up to a vine and realized his thirst. He gazed longingly at the fat, purple, overripe grapes. He placed his front paws against the trunk of the vine, stretched his neck, and reached for the fruit, but it was too high. Irritated, he tried again and launched himself upward, but his jaw snapped only at fresh air. With a third attempt, he leapt with all his might and landed on his back on the hard ground. The grapes were unmoved. The fox turned up his nose and said, "These aren't even ripe yet. Why would I want sour grapes?" Holding his head high, he rode back into the forest.

Rolf Deobelli in *The Art of Thinking Clearly* explained that the fox can resolve the conflict in one of three ways: 1) by somehow getting at the grapes, 2) by admitting that his skills are insufficient, or 3) by reinterpreting what happened retrospectively—a cognitive dissonance reaction.

A respected hand surgeon was operating on a small bone in the wrist called the scaphoid that was broken into two pieces. The first goal of the surgery was to determine if the bone was viable or had adequate blood supply and capacity to heal. This particular bone starts out disadvantaged with poor blood supply, and its unpredictable healing following fracture is well-recognized in orthopaedic medicine. If it were not viable, it would have to be removed and discarded. If it were viable, it would be fixed with screws.

As the surgeon manipulated the bone to assess its viability, it slipped free of its ligaments, slipped free of the clamp holding it, and popped out of the wrist and hit the floor, thus becoming contaminated and creating significant risk of infection if it were to be placed back into the wrist. The room became uncomfortably silent with assistants and nursing staff in a true pause mode. The surgeon hesitated for a moment and then simply declared that the bone was not viable and therefore could be discarded. Everyone in the room, including the anesthesiologist, could feel what could have been a surgeon's flurry of frustration and anger completely washed away with a simple "the bone was dead."

I was assisting an ankle fracture surgery as a resident. The surgery was being performed by a senior surgeon regarded as having way above average surgical skill. A fractured bone fragment called the medial malleolus, on the inside part of the ankle, was rotated abnormally and the surgeon was performing releases of ligaments and tissue with a scalpel. I observed the surgeon accidently cut a major tendon in the foot called the posterior tibial tendon. (Without the tendon working properly, the arch of your foot can collapse into a flat foot.) The slice of the tendon was in the same direction as the scalpel dissection movements and had no features of abrasion at the edges or other features of trauma. The fracture edge, which often has a sharp edge like broken glass, was perpendicular to the cut in the tendon—meaning it was not realistic that the fracture edge could have cut the tendon. Despite the obvious physical cutting of it with the scalpel, the fact that the cut was in a different direction than the fracture fragment (yes, if this were a *Law and Order* episode, the coroner could testify that the scalpel had to have cut the tendon), the surgeon proclaimed, and even expressed amazement, that the fracture had cut the tendon. He even stated that, in 20 years of treating these injuries, he had never seen a medial malleolus fracture cut the posterior tibial tendon. To this day, I believe the surgeon honestly believes he did not cut the tendon. That is how powerful the mind is.

Surgeons deal with bad outcomes in different ways. Most physician malpractice lawsuits stem from a failure to recognize complications or diagnoses that then cause delay in treatment or incorrect treatment. Joseph T. Hallinan in *Why We Make Mistakes* revealed that, in the United States, between 44,000 and 98,000 patients are believed to die each year from preventable medical errors. Hallinan describes operating rooms as being extremely different than the atmosphere of commercial airline cockpits with regard to attitude. ORs are hierarchical, with the surgeon on top. Alternatively, cockpits are not. Flight crews, which consist of a captain, first officer, and a second officer, are encouraged to speak up if they see something amiss, irrespective of rank. Everyone is equal when it comes to exposing potential errors.

Ego is, apparently, higher in some occupations than others. A survey, given to tens of thousands of pilots and doctors and other healthcare workers in the Unites States, Europe, and Israel, was extremely revealing. In response to the question of whether junior staff members should be free to question decisions made by senior staff members, 97 percent of airline pilots said yes while only 55 percent of surgeons said yes. Pilots also were far more willing to acknowledge their limitations. In response to the survey statement: "Even when fatigued, I perform effectively during critical times: 70 percent of surgeons agreed with the statement, but only 26 percent of pilots concurred.

I recently posed a question in a morbidity and mortality conference where surgeons gather to analyze their mistakes with an effort to avoid them in the future. These conferences are restricted and confidential. A case was presented by a fellow where screws were placed incorrectly into the joint which could cause rapid joint destruction. This required the patient to be taken back to the operating room for a second surgery to correct the poorly positioned screws. The OR started at 7 a.m. that day (as it does every day). This surgery with the complication began at 8 p.m. that evening—13 hours after the day's first operation, following several energy-depleting prior surgeries. I posed the question of fatigue as a factor for the mistaken screw placement in the setting of such a long day of operating. The fellow who participated in the surgery and who had to present the complication to the team of surgeons in the audience stated that he did not feel fatigue was a factor. Later, however, in discussing the case further with the fellow, he changed his opinion and did conclude that fatigue was a factor.

Josh Kaufman in *Personal MBA* described analytical honesty as dispassionately measuring and analyzing the data you have. We intrinsically care deeply about how others perceive us and, therefore, are incentivized to make things look better than they are. These biases are extremely costly to the development of a surgeon.

This feature of individuals can be applied to systems and hospitals. Amy Edmondson, the Novartis Professor of Leadership and Management at the Harvard Business School, discovered something surprising: the best-run hospitals reported *10 times* more errors than the poorly run hospitals. Investigating further, Edmondson found that the real difference wasn't in making mistakes (all the hospitals made about the same amount). The difference was in *reporting* them. Well-run hospitals operated in an open, transparent manner; mistakes were seen as opportunities for discussion and improvement. Poorly-run hospitals, on the other hand, were filled with fear, uncertainty, and silence. Employees thought that "heads would roll" if they admitted making mistakes. In other words, the better hospitals weren't necessarily smarter or more talented. They had something more powerful: a psychological safe zone; a shared place where mistakes weren't hidden, but discussed in the clear light of day.

Joe Girardi, who wore number 27 and managed the Yankees to their 27th world championship, accepted my invitation to come speak at a hospital leadership meeting. This was a pep rally held in January to kick off the year and inspire the various leaders of different clinical departments, such as Radiology, Patient Services, and Endocrinology. Joe gave a heartwarming narrative of his personal experience with doctors and with illness in his family. The approximately 1,000 employees in attendance were encouraged to ask him questions. He was asked "How would you advise us who are leading groups of physicians and other healthcare staff to improve our performance?" His answer was immediate, "In the Yankees organization, we have a team of all-stars much like the staff you have at your hospital. To get the players to work toward the goal of the team and win a championship, every player must leave his ego at the entrance to the stadium. Ego is the biggest obstacle to team performance when the team has all-stars."

How do I handle personal cognitive dissonance? I create an environment where *making mistakes and talking about them is okay*. I treat mistakes as a learning opportunity and not as a declaration of the skill of a surgeon. I tell myself regularly, that if a member of the team offers a suggestion, to consider the merits of it before rejecting it, especially when emotions are high because the surgery is going poorly.

People who are serious about learning from errors understand and manage cognitive dissonance with brutal analytical honesty.

Leave your ego at the door and make self-critique your most powerful surgical mastery tool.

30

Mistakes are building blocks for growth.

When you reach the sweet spot on the edge of your ability and go beyond it, you're reforming the strengthening new connections in your brain. Mistakes aren't really mistakes. They're the information you use to build the right links. The more you pay attention to the mistake and fix it, the more of the correct connections you'll build inside your brain.

As illustrated in the previous tip, most of us are allergic to mistakes. When we make one, our instinct is to look away, ignore it, and pretend it didn't happen. This is a mistake in itself because mistakes are our guideposts for improvement. Brain scan studies reveal a vital moment 0.25 seconds after a mistake is made, people do one of two things: they look hard at the mistake or they ignore it. People who pay deeper attention to an error learn significantly more than those who don't. Address mistakes immediately and take them seriously, but never personally. Visualizing the process as it happens helps you reinterpret mistakes as what they actually are: tools for building skills.

Learn as much as possible from every mistake. The mistakes are there even if you do not see them. Look for them, and then visualize them. Convert the negative energy—mistakes—into positive action. In surgery, clearly, it's better not to make the mistake. But, as in learning to play the guitar, the aim is to repeat the proper technique and then feel how it is to be wrong again, and then continue the correct way.

Cherish your greatest tool for improvement—your mistakes.

31

Develop a positive mindset (mistakes and failure).

Michael Jordan publicly embraced failure in a Nike commercial that states "I've missed more than 9,000 shots. I've lost almost 300 games, and 26 times, I've been trusted to take the game-winning shot and missed." This embrace of failure is testament to the positive mindset. Carol Dweck, a Professor of Psychology at Stanford University who studies motivation, performed an experiment in which she used a questionnaire to determine if sixth graders had a fixed mindset of believing one is born with talent and intelligence, or a growth mindset of believing one can acquire intelligence with effort. The subjects were given problems and puzzles with increasing difficulty. The growth mindset blew the fixed mindset away when it came to the difficult ones, in part, because the fixed mindset people avoid challenges. A growth mindset believes that properly applied effort leads to achievement. I hit an obstacle as a freshman soccer player at Columbia University. I was playing at

Baker field on the upper tip of Manhattan when I became intimidated by some of the older, more skillful players. In addition, the senior players could smell insecurity and had zero tolerance for players who could not execute. I began to avoid getting free to receive the ball.

I then analyzed what I could do to improve my performance and enjoyment. It was as simple as recognizing that I had an opportunity to play at a high level with some of the best collegiate players in the country. Why wouldn't I want the ball every time I could get it to show what I could do and enjoy playing like when I was a kid in the backyard? Why not embrace the opportunity? Why fear failure? Derek Jeter has told teammates who are slumping to simply go out to the plate, forget about the critical fans and reporters, have fun, and stop worrying about failure. In fact, in Jeter's post-game interview on his last home game of his career, he stated he was wishing the ball would not be hit to him at short. This was in response to the intense emotion he was feeling at the start of his last game. The game unfolded with him getting a walk off hit to win the game— September 25, 2014. Despite the emotion of a career-ending game, he clearly managed his last game with his own advice to avoid fear of failure and concentrate on opportunity—and to just have fun.

Surgeons must maintain a positive mindset, accept the possibility of failure, lose the fear of failure when operating, and celebrate success. Surgeons must embrace failure and learn from every mistake as opposed to feeling that a failure has defined them. Jeter maintains a positive growth mindset and embraces failure by entering every situation with an intensity and concentration to perform optimally and remembering to always have fun at the plate rather than have negative thoughts of striking out. Do surgeons have the equivalent of a Derek Jeter fist pump after a strong defensive play, or hand clap as he rounds first with a base hit? Yes.

To grow you must get positive and stay positive.

32

Choose blue-collar surgical training.

Luxury reduces effort. Talent hotbeds around the world are often far from luxurious. Simple, humble spaces that focus attention on the deep-practice tasks at hand: reaching, repeating, and struggling. As a kid, I recalled wanting the fanciest soccer jerseys for Sunday games. Stripes. Two tones. In college, we used cotton T-shirts with a number on it. Why? Work ethic and deliberate practice stands out and is stimulated more and to a higher degree. It even put fear into other teams.

Many developing surgeons would like residency training in a "plush environment": technicians to run the intraoperative live x-ray device, a blood drawing team, physician assistants to take care of mundane patient responsibilities. My training involved no such amenities. On my first day on ob-gyn service as a medical student, I was shown once how to draw blood on a patient. The next day and for the next six weeks, I drew blood on all 28 patients on the ob-gyn service, beginning at 4:30 a.m., to get done in time for 6 a.m. rounds. As an orthopaedic resident, we checked every item of equipment prior to the start of a surgery and ran the x-ray c-arm ourselves during the procedure (you trained yourself how to use the c-arm on the fly). This practice created thoughtful competence with a "work and do" ethic rather than an observational process. Surgeons who train with passive observation in luxury environments regress compared to the accelerating power of active preparation and increased responsibility that is part of more Spartan environments.

From a distance, top performers seem to live charmed, cushy lives. When you look closer, however, you'll find they spend vast portions of their time practicing their craft. Their mindset is not entitled or arrogant; it's 100 percent blue-collar. They get up in the morning and go to work every day, whether they feel like it or not.

We had dirty scrubs, had just put a cast on, just debrided (cleaned out) an open wound. Now we have cast techs, wound care teams, and long white coats. Take pride in effortful achievement rather than celebrating a leisure, plush environment.

Choose the harder path if you wish to pursue excellence.

33

Pull it apart in the lab—do research.

I do a lot of research, which can greatly enhance one's curriculum vitae, application, and even soften the interview by generating interesting topics to discuss. I am frequently asked why I do so much research. I have a simple answer, "It makes me a better surgeon."

Sports medicine surgery is most often designed to correct a muscle, tendon, or ligament that has been damaged. The success of the surgery depends on whether the new fixed body part can stand up to the test of activity. Can the ACL reconstruction stay intact following a hit from a 280-pound linebacker? Our success is measured on whether our surgeries fail. Much of the research I have done involves pulling something apart. This is a completely unique opportunity. The research involves subjecting the knee to loads that would make it fail. The failure is observed, the loads measured, the initiating point of the failure, and whether it is the graft that fails or the implant that fails. The experimentation can be done to vary parameters to find out if one implant is superior to another, or if placing the graft in one position is superior to another position.

I recently took care of a Division I collegiate running back who had an ACL reconstruction. In his first game returning from injury, he re-tore his graft. In a clinical situation such as this, it is impossible to observe the graft failing during the injury. But the knowledge gained from observing how it typically fails in the lab is a tremendous asset.

In business, Josh Kaufman has referred to this type of analysis as stress testing. "What would it take to break what you have built?" Kaufman observed that each time he launched his reading list on his website, his web server would go down. He upgraded several times but, with each launch, the server crashed. Instead of simply trying to solve the problem with theorized solutions and crossed fingers during each launch, he got serious about stress testing. He tried to break the system intentionally by simulating large traffic to the site and experimented with different approaches until zeroing in on a solution.

I have tested the muscles that assist the stability of the elbow and protect the MCL. I know now which muscles must be well protected during surgical procedures. To further study Tommy John Surgery to improve baseball players with the injury, I performed the surgery on cadavers and then pulled the elbows apart with a machine while observing how the reconstruction falls apart. There is no other way to observe what exactly is happening to the ligament when it fails. Based on the weak link that always failed first, I changed the surgical technique, greatly increasing the strength of the reconstruction—and developed a better surgery. This, then, changes the way I practice and do surgery, and it has only happened because of time spent in a research lab.

I began testing surgical procedures in the Columbia Orthopaedic Research in 1988 as an undergraduate mechanical engineering student. I am now the Director of Biomechanics research at that same laboratory.

Test something to get better at it.

34

Chunking can unleash magical improvisation.

We have all witnessed jaw-dropping athletic feats that defy even elite performance. Some believe it starts with roots in repetition. Repetition has a bad reputation. We tend to think of it as dull and uninspiring. Repetition, however, is the single most powerful instrument we have to improve our skills, because it uses the built-in mechanism for making the wires of our brains run faster and more accurately. Embracing repetition means changing your mindset; instead of viewing it as a chore, view it as your single most powerful tool.

In prior tips, we emphasized repetition must be combined with reaching, finding the sweet spot where you work just beyond your comfort zone for rapid skill acquisition. Here, we are discussing repetition of a subset of connected skills to make them stick and become automatic. While practicing guitar to master a new song, for example, I will focus on a small section and play it repeatedly until I can get through it without a mistake. Once I get it, I play it again a few times, repeating it to make it stick and become automatic. I move to another section and play it until I can play it without a mistake. I repeat it to make it stick. Once I can play the whole song without mistakes, the parts I struggled with I don't have to consciously think about any more. My mind becomes free to work on playing the song with certain stylistic points such as sustaining and emphasizing particular notes.

Visualize a flow chart that indicates repetition leading to automaticity, which then facilitates deeper thinking, and perception, which then facilitates improved execution and creativity. For an experienced fighter pilot, it means seeing several moves ahead in a dog fight. For athletes, it allows them to see things before they happen. It is often referred to as *game sense*. Athletes even use the term "playing unconscious."

In soccer, elite players perceive the field and understand the flow of the game and exploit weakness. These are soft skills leading to exceptional improvisation and deserve expanded analysis. Top performers can filter out the unimportant and weight the important and situational information. Chunking refers to mastering subsets of skills which go on to become automatic. I have taken a shower and washed my hair while deeply thinking about the day's upcoming tasks (most often the surgeries for that day). While still in the shower, I often can't remember if I washed my hair because the chunking process, in this case, hair washing, converted to an unconscious process.

Derek Jeter has captivated fans countless times, but one particular play demonstrated deeper knowledge and skill than any other in baseball. With two outs in the bottom of the seventh in Game 3 of the 2001 American League Division Series, the Yankees lead 1-0. Mike Mussina delivers a pitch to Jeremy Giambi who singles to right. Terrence Long then slashes a ball down the first-base line passing the reach of Yankees first baseman Tino Martinez. Giambi rounds third base and sees third-base coach Ron Washington waving wildly to take it home. Shane Spencer tracks down the ball and Alfonso Soriano sprints into short right field for the cutoff. Martinez is at the first-base bag, backing up Soriano.

Derek Jeter is the shortstop and is *reading* the play.

Spencer hurls the ball for a play at the plate but the throw is off line and it sails over Soriano's and Martinez's head. Giambi senses an easy scoring opportunity. Suddenly, and out of nowhere, Jeter appears darting from the middle of the infield and arrives at the end of the Spencer errant throw. Derek Jeter had no business being there, no business at all. That's what made the play so astounding.

Jeter scoops up the ball on a bounce with two hands along the baseline. With his momentum carrying him off the field and toward the Yankees' dugout, he somehow flips the ball backhanded, 20 feet to his right.

"I didn't have time to turn around, set up and throw," Jeter told the press afterwards, as if the play were simply routine. "Basically, I just got rid of it. If I tried to spin around, he would have been safe." As Giambi comes chugging home, Hernandez, doing what the on-deck hitter is supposed to do when there is a play at the plate, signals for Giambi to slide. He yells. He waves. But Giambi doesn't look for him, doesn't see him, illustrating his poor base running fundamentals and instincts. "The stadium was so loud, he couldn't hear me yell, so I just put my hand out and told him to go down," Hernandez would say later.

Meanwhile, Jeter's backhand flip is so accurate that Posada needs only to reach back and simply tag out Giambi. When Posada reaches to catch the ball, he swipes at Giambi with his glove. Giambi, who should have slid into home plate, goes in standing up. Posada's tag gets Giambi's right foot just as it is about to come down on home plate. Giambi tries leaping over Posada's tag. He's unsuccessful, and Kerwin Danley, the home-plate umpire, calls him out.

Jeter thrusts his arm in the air. Posada leaps in the air. Yankees all over the field and in the dugout celebrate. Teams, of course, do not practice plays where they have a third relay man. There are double cutoff men and if someone overthrows it, it's the catcher picking up the ball, not the shortstop. But that's Jeter for you. "We're probably never going to see that play ever again," A's third baseman Eric Chavez says today.

"A shortstop making that play behind first base, in foul territory, then flipping the ball to the catcher with his momentum carrying him away from the play—it's unheard of."

Do surgeons have the equivalent of a playoff game with two outs and a capacity to magically correct an uncorrectable situation? YES.

When you repeat ACL surgery, distal biceps repair, patella ligament surgery, and Tommy John Surgery—at a certain point—it all clicks. Many teachers of surgery call it the "aha" moment. When developing surgeons recognize that principles applied to each surgery actually are similar, the chunking then begins to work on a much more global scale. While you may not have performed the same number of repetitions for a distal biceps surgery, the complication of drilling into the bone and finding the bone has crumbling on the back wall of the tunnel can be managed the same for distal biceps surgery as for an ACL reconstruction.

Furthermore, if the steps and features of the surgery are chunked and automatic, your mind has the ability to wander and look ahead for trouble and then adjust to avoid it. Jeter saw the play developing and somehow perceived more than anyone on the field that an overthrow was about to happen and he could correct it. Surgeons who have chunked operations can perceive more and correct mistakes before they happen or correct them without consequence. Patients would be shocked to know that these game-type situations occur in surgery frequently and are often the aspects of surgery that separate great surgeons from truly great surgeons.

Young firefighters, when engaged in a fire, are concentrating on their gear and trying not to deviate from exact protocols. For experienced fire fighters, the protocol is second nature and they do not need to concentrate on their gear because they have automated or chunked those processes from years of repetition. Their minds are free to explore the fire in more detail. They can perceive more, and make better decisions on how to fight the fire. As an example, a senior firefighter saw that, despite his team hitting the base of the building fire with water, the fire was not extinguishing as had happened repeatedly in his career. Knowing something was not right, he ordered all the firefighters out of the building and, seconds later, the floor collapsed. It turned out, the fire was also on the floor below and his experience and ability to see beyond targeting water and proper use of equipment and protocols allowed him to demonstrate features we observe in elite athletes.

Chunking in surgery can have profound benefits just as in fighting fires. In performing a new surgery for the first time that required complex placement of sutures to fix a fractured bone in the shoulder (called a bony bankart procedure), I could see that, several steps further into the surgery, tying the sutures was going to create problems for passing the next sutures and continuing with the surgery. I did not have to actually make the mistake because of the ability to see several steps ahead, much like a chess player sees moves before they are played. Other surgeons, after trying this operation repeatedly with difficulty, have since asked me how to manage the difficulty with the sutures.

Chunking can lead to creativity. Creativity in solving problems as related in surgery and firefighting is well-recognized in the greatest sports talents. Doug Lemon, in *Practice Perfect,* posits that Johan Cruyoff was the most imaginative player ever to play soccer. His rationale was that he had superb hard skills that did not deteriorate under pressure or fatigue. Since he did not have to concern himself with conscious thoughts of how to manage the ball at his feet, even with extreme pressure from his opponents, his mind was free to be creative. Drilling to mastery facilitates creativity.

Chunking can lead to deeper appreciation. When hitting a baseball, average players will look at the ball. Better players look at the hips, shoulders, and arms of the pitcher. They can predict how the ball is going to be pitched even prior to the ball release. This enables top performers to know what's going to happen better than average performers. These players chunk the entire movement of their opponent. In tennis, waiting to return a serve; at the plate in baseball; watching pitchers or servers position their hips, shoulders and arms, there is not enough time to react to the ball and the spin without the early information telegraphed by the pitcher's or server's movement. In squash, great players can see the other player's position and movement and can begin to move to where the ball is going. This is on an unconscious level.

NFL coach Tony Dungy took the opposite approach from most coaches who believe that complicated schemes win games. Dungy believed the opposite; he simply wanted his team to be faster than their opponents. To accomplish this, he taught his players only a handful of plays, but had them practice those plays over and over again until the behaviors were automatic. The result was that his players didn't need to think as much during a game and could rely on their ingrained habits. This gave Dungy's players a small, but significant, advantage. They were faster than their opponents because they eliminated the time needed for decision-making.

Tony Dungy explains, "Champions don't do extraordinary things. They do ordinary things, but they do them without thinking, too fast for the other team to react. They follow the habits they've learned."

Exceptional surgeons, athletes, and, actually any performer, attain the level of mystical excellence by using the chunking process.

35

Close your eyes and visualize. One of the quickest ways to deepen practice is also one of the simplest: Close your eyes. Musicians have long used this technique to improve feel and accuracy, but it also works for other skills. Michael Jordan practiced free throws with his eyes shut; Navy SEAL training includes a generous helping of pitch-black darkness during which soldiers learn to disassemble and reassemble their weapons, and, cooperate to pitch a tent. The reason, in each case, is the same. Closing your eyes is a swift way to nudge you to the edges of your ability; to get you into your sweet spot. It sweeps away distraction and engages your other senses to provide new feedback. It helps to engrave the blueprint of a task on your brain.

While a surgeon would never purposefully operate with his eyes closed, or in a dark operating room. I often close my door, close my eyes, and visualize a surgery mentally, like a musician feeling the execution of a song. Feel the surgery while doing it with your eyes closed.

Visualization is simply mental rehearsal. You create images in your mind of having or doing whatever it is you want, and can do the exercise repeatedly.

Arnold Schwarzenegger has argued, "It's all in the mind." Arnold can remember when he had little else except a belief that his mind was the key to getting where he wanted to go. "The mind is really so incredible. Before I won my first Mr. Universe title, I walked around the tournament like I owned it. I had won it so many times in my mind, the title was already mine. Then when I moved on to the movies I used the same technique. I visualized daily being a successful actor and earning big money."

I have a habit that, at times, I wish I could turn off. Just before falling asleep, I play a mental movie of the next day's surgical performance. Not only for an individual surgery, but for six to eight, sometimes 10, surgeries being done the next day. I rehearse and trouble-shoot each surgery for problems—equipment, execution issues, my assistants, anesthesia, post-op management, etc.

I run two operating rooms. I rehearse before I go to bed with the lights out and alarm set. I do it in sequence. *Room 10: JS (we refer to patients often by initials to keep anonymity) minor league player, New York Yankees, medial meniscus tear. Plan—no tourniquet. Room 11: college freshman with posterior labral tear batting. Plan—knotless anchor repair with post op brace placed in external rotation,* and so on, until I'm done with all the cases. Top performers, ranging from athletes to comedians, visualize their idealized performance in their heads. Research supports this idea, linking visualization to improved performance, motivation, mental toughness, and confidence. Treat it as a way to rev the engine of your unconscious mind, so it spends more time churning toward your goals. I have, on occasion, not performed this and have regretted my lack of confidence the next day.

Just before you sleep, watch a mental movie of your next day's performance.

36

To achieve true mastery—teach it.

When instructing a skill, you come to understand it more deeply. When you see someone struggle and help them through it, you improve your ability to deal with personal struggles. Teaching surgery has a great impact on personal surgical mastery. All surgeons teach, coach, or mentor others. This teaching is delivered to residents, fellows, support staff, but most importantly, patients and their families.

When I studied mechanical engineering at Columbia University, I began working with a PhD candidate graduate student while I was an undergraduate. He now is a full professor of mechanical engineering and has explained to me his preparation for a three-hour lecture usually takes 10 hours. The process of teaching a procedure involves breaking the procedure down into parts, finding ways to explain each part, and anticipating the challenges a student will face in mastering it. Students ask questions and probe teachers building an understanding that is much greater than required of simple competence. What may have been natural to me, but is a problem for a student, creates new questions and thoughts which lead to much deeper understanding for the teacher.

During my training at Columbia University, we spent several months at Harlem Hospital. The orthopaedic team was comprised of three attendings and three residents. We took care of a large number of patients and were extremely busy—every third day we worked straight through the day, all through the night, and all the next day—36 hours straight was typical. While in my third year of training, I was, in fact, the chief resident at Harlem Hospital and that meant I was responsible for all the patients. I would review all the injuries presented to the emergency room and review the x-ray interpretations and best treatments for each injury with the second-year residents. To be able to teach the other second-year residents who are in their first year of orthopaedic training comprised several features. The motivation to be competent to teach was amazing. You study a lot to teach yourself, you practice and study 50 times harder to teach someone else. The second feature of teaching is seeing deeper into every problem, so that if a resident could not grasp the concept, you could present it in a different way, break it down into smaller pieces, or relate it to another principle.

I found a similar strategy presented by Josh Kaufman in *Personal MBA* by Talking Aloud Partner Problem-Solving (TAPPS). This is a teaching/learning strategy that requires pairing people, with one designated as the problem solver and the other as monitor. The monitor's job is to listen, but not contribute any advice about the problem and its solution. She can alert the problem solver to his own thinking pattern by saying, for example, "I heard you mention a potential obstacle to solving the problem earlier, but then I didn't hear more about that." But she can't add, "I see a couple of other obstacles that you didn't talk about." Monitoring comments are exclusively about the designated problem solver's talking aloud process. Generally, increased problem-solving speed and efficiency resulted when the pairs group was compared with a control group. When teaching to students or anyone—they essentially are serving as a monitor by probing with questions. Students often can uncover deficiencies in your (the teacher's) understanding of concepts.

I have written more than 100 articles on the step-by-step technique to perform sports medicine surgical procedures such as an ACL reconstruction, or to repair a shoulder that has repeatedly dislocated. In fact, I have written 50 articles related to MCL reconstruction of the elbow or the Tommy John Surgery. Writing all of these articles forced me to think of each surgery and component of surgery more deeply, which is analogous to formal teaching

Skill competence has been described in psychology as a four-stage progression. The theory was developed by Noel Burch in the 1970s. It also has been attributed to Abraham Maslow, although the model does not appear in his major works. It applies to surgeons and many, perhaps all, aspects of skill development. Initially, surgeons are unaware of how little they know, or unconscious of their incompetence. As they recognize their incompetence, they consciously acquire skills, then consciously use them. Eventually, any skill can be utilized without it being consciously thought through: the individual is said to have then acquired unconscious competence. The summary below provides more detail.

1) UNCONSCIOUS INCOMPETENCE

The surgeon is so early in the process that s/he is unaware of the magnitude of his or her deficiency.

2) CONSCIOUS INCOMPETENCE

The surgeon becomes aware s/he does not understand or know how to do something. S/he also begins to recognize the deficit and becomes motivated to learn the new skills to gain competence. Making mistakes is frequent and may be central to the learning process at this stage, as the surgeon refines the skills through practice.

3) CONSCIOUS COMPETENCE

The surgeon understands or knows how to do something. S/he can demonstrate the skill or knowledge, but it requires concentration and effort. It may need to be broken down into steps or detailed processes. There often is heavy conscious involvement in executing the new skill. The surgeon understands the obstacles to acquire the skill and often is a good teacher at this level.

4) UNCONSCIOUS COMPETENCE

The surgeon has had so much refining practice with a skill that s/he does not really need to think about what to do. It has become "second nature" and can be performed with very low frequency of errors. Because the skill is not occupying much of the individual's conscious thoughts, it can often be performed while executing another task. The surgeon has become so comfortable with the skill s/he will often be able to teach it to others.

Teaching uncovers how much you still may need to learn. American journalist Sydney J. Harris wrote, "A winner knows how much he still has to learn, even when he is considered an expert by others. A loser wants to be considered as an expert by others before he has learned enough to know how little he knows."

Teach and enjoy your personal improvement as well as your students.

37

Be a better coach. Daniel Coyle, in *The Little Book of Talent*, outlines six pieces of advice for effective coaching that easily apply to surgical training.

1) Use the first few seconds to connect on an emotional level.

When you recall your most influential teachers and coaches, your memories are likely more related to the way that person made you feel, rather than what that person did. Coaches need to find what is special in their students, understand them, and develop trust.

2) Avoid giving long speeches—instead, deliver vivid chunks of information.

Long, dramatic, inspirational speeches by coaches are more effective in movies than real life. Master teachers and coaches do not stand in front; they stand *next* to their students. They deliver short packets of information in vibrant pieces.

3) Be allergic to mushy language.

Coaches should avoid the mistake of using soft, imprecise communication. Consider a Little League player at the plate whose coach says, "Move your hands higher." The player makes an adjustment but does not make the coach happy. The language is too vague and does not state how high, e.g., "to the shoulders, above the head."

To avoid this, use language that is concrete and specific. For example:

"Your outlined incision is too low" is vague. "Start the incision three fingerbreadths below the medial joint line" is concrete.

"The operating table is too low" is vague "Raise the table until it reaches the same level as your umbilicus (belly button)" is concrete.

"Get anesthesia on board" is vague. "Contact anesthesia and explain the graft will be harvested from the leg for the elbow reconstruction and, therefore, general anesthesia will be required in addition to an upper extremity nerve block" is concrete.

4) Make a scorecard for your students.

Life is full of scorecards: sales figures, performance rankings, test scores, tournament results. The problem with those cards is they can distort priorities that lead us toward short-term outcomes and away from the learning process. We've all seen it happen in business and in sports organizations that focus maniacally on the results of the day. They tend to lose sight of the larger opportunity for learning and developing competencies for the long run.

Create your own scorecard. Take a metric that measures the skills you want to develop and start keeping track. In business, they call the scorecard "key performance indicators." In sports, for example, in an effort to create greater passing proficiency, soccer coaches track the number of smart passes. Teammates use this number, not the score, as the most accurate measure of their team's success and growth. The players catch on and try to exceed themselves each game. Regardless of what happens on the scoreboard, the smart pass number gives them an accurate way to measure their real progress. In surgery, metrics for residents are often how far s/he can get into the case before the attending has to intervene to correct a problem or get the surgery back on track.

5) Maximize reach fullness.

Reach fullness is the essence of learning. It happens when the learner is leaning forward, stretching, struggling, and improving. The best teachers and coaches design situations that force students into an active state from a passive state. Some progressive schools increased reach fullness through a technique called "flipping the classroom." The term refers to changing the traditional model, in which students spend class time listening to a lecture and then do reinforcement work at home. In a flipped classroom, the students do the reverse. They listen to lectures at home, online, and spend class time actively struggling with the work: doing problems, wrestling with concepts, in essence, reaching, while the teacher walks around with a coaching style, and helps individuals one at a time. In a year-long study of algebra students at one California high school, students in a flipped classroom scored 23 percent higher on tests than students in the conventional classroom.

The larger point is that being a good teacher means thinking like a designer. Ask yourself: What kind of space will create the most reaching environment? How can you replace moments of passivity with moments of active learning?

6) Aim to create independent learners.

Your long-term goal as the teacher, coach, or mentor is to help your learners so much they no longer need you. To do this, avoid becoming the center of attention. Instead, create an environment where people can keep reaching on their own. Whenever possible, step away and create moments of independence. Think of your job as building a little master coach chip in their brain, a tiny version of you, guiding them as they go forward.

To give our fellows in training an independent environment, I have chosen—after their first six months of training—to assume my job in the patient clinic while I observe them. My job is to review each patient who is evaluated by residents, verify the history and exam, interpret the X-ray and MRI, obtain the most accurate diagnosis, and create the most appropriate treatment plan for each patient, which educates the residents. The fellow who steps into this role has great learning potential. I often think of it as the grandmaster chess player who can play six chess games simultaneously with six different opponents as numerous residents present their cases simultaneously.

Daniel Coyle wrote that how feedback is delivered from a coach or teacher is the most critical aspect of advancement or regression. Frequently, the coach thinks the quality of the information is what's most important. Coyle revealed that to be false.

A team of psychologists from Stanford, Yale, Columbia, and elsewhere investigated instructor feedback. They had middle-school teachers assign an essay to their students, after which students were given various types of feedback. Amazingly, one type of feedback improved student effort and performance to a degree significantly different than the others. It was deemed "magical." Students who received this feedback chose to revise their paper 40 to 320 percent more often than students who did not. The "magic" in 19 words:

I'm giving you these comments because
I have very high expectations and I know
that you can reach them.

This statement establishes trust, standards, and belief. It acknowledges the endeavor is far from easy, yet creates sincere belief that it can be done.

Coach with excellence to achieve your personal pursuit of greatness. Every person you coach is a mirror for you.

———————

38

Praise effortful practice, not good

results. In an amazing praise experiment performed by Carol Dweck, PhD, a group of fifth graders were given a series of puzzles to work on. Afterwards, the students were given their scores and six words of praise, either "You must be smart at this!" or "You must have worked really hard." Remarkable results ensued. All students were given a second test and given a choice of whether they wanted to take a hard test or an easy test. A full two-thirds of students praised for intelligence took the easy test. Ninety percent of effort-praised kids took the hard test. They all then took a very difficult test. The effort-praised group tried harder. Now, the kicker: They took the initial test that started the experiment. The intelligence-praised group declined in performance compared to the first time they took the test, even though it was an identical test. The effort-praised group increased their scores 30 percent.

The kids were then told that the same study was being done at another school and that the children there might like to hear from students who had already taken the test. She gave the students a sheet on which they could record their thoughts along with a space where they could record how many problems they got right. Children praised for effort told the truth almost always; the group praised for intelligence lied 40 percent of the time. Doing well is so important they felt compelled to distort their performance to their peers.

As surgical educators, we praise results, as poor performance is not tolerated. Surgery does not have expressions like "You'll get 'em next time." Fixed mindset/intelligence-praised individuals don't deal with complications well. Patients always praise their surgeon for their result, not for their hard work. What differs for some centers of excellence is the quality of the teaching attitude. The kids at Florida's Nick Bollettieri Tennis Academy crave practice and hard work. He praises effort, never talent. He never criticizes mistakes. He uses them as opportunities to learn. A constant environment of discipline and effort-praise creates a growth mindset.

Early praise also can create complacency or even fear of underachieving or failing to meet expectations, which thereby undermines the process of reaching. Praise must celebrate effort, not results. The quest for talent requires a marathon approach in terms of dedication, with many smaller sprints within the marathon. Some athletes develop a fixed mindset: they either have it or they don't, or they assign blame to their perceived misfortunes. A player who hates the coach, typically, has a skill problem and blames the coach rather than himself. Jim Collins describes Level 5 leaders as those who always look within in the context of a failed objective. A weak leader blames a myriad of victims, such as an assistant or, sometimes, even the weather, for the undesired outcome.

I consciously create a plan for when things are not going well during a complicated surgery. This is the time to praise and treat everyone in the room respectfully. So many frustrated surgeons blame the support staff, which creates negativity and in so many ways that further compromises the surgery.

Give praise with skill and effectiveness.

39

Cultivate your grit. Grit is the Holy Grail for achievement—in any endeavor. Grit is the mix of passion, perseverance, and self-discipline that keeps us moving forward in spite of obstacles. It's not flashy. It's not seductive. It's not clever. Despite the distraction of sparkly displays of skill, grit is what makes the difference in the long run. When you hit an obstacle, how do you react? Examine the places in your life where you persevered, and celebrate them in yourself and others.

We all fall down. Surgeons have complications, poor outcomes, and receive criticism—essentially disappointments that can attack your self-confidence. How you respond to this adversity is one of the most predictive traits of future accomplishment. This feature of grit can by identified as early as childhood.

Historically, surgical training has been an abusive process, perhaps, to build resilience or select out the trainees without resilience. As a resident, I was once asked by a fellow to give one of my attendings' patients a medicine called Inderal, which is a blood pressure medicine. When I met with the patient in between surgeries I assisted with, the patient told me he had no issues with blood pressure. I discussed this with the fellow, who was not concerned. So I called a cardiology consult, who agreed the patient did not need Inderal. The attending came later to see the patient and saw that I had not given his patient the medicine he requested. The medicine was Indocin. The fellow misunderstood the attending's instructions.

The next day, the attending publicly scolded me and, without an opportunity to explain, he threatened that my poor performance would no longer be tolerated. The fellow never took responsibility to let anyone know he gave me incorrect instruction. I learned how to be resilient to abusive surgical training experiences. Be resilient to bad outcomes. Mariano Rivera is well known for his ability to accept the responsibility of a blown save. He will take every question from every reporter. He is also known not to let it affect his next save opportunity.

Albert Einstein said, "It's not that I'm so smart; it's just that I stay with problems longer." John C. Norcross, clinical psychologist and professor at the University of Scranton, studies goals and success and believes the characteristic that best distinguishes who reaches their goals from those who don't: expectations. Both types of people experience the same amount of failure early in the process. Members of the successful group don't expect to succeed right away, and they view their failures as a reason to recommit and a reminder to refocus on their goals with more determination. My motto with my own children and those I coach is simple: "Never give up." If you are wrestling, you must never quit simply when you are tired, you quit when your opponent is tired.

Grit is not always possessed by those who you think would have it. I have observed grit in true underdogs. My alma mater mascot is an example. My recruitment to Columbia's soccer team began in 1985, the year they had a Division I undefeated regular season and made the biggest stage in American soccer at the time—the NCAA Division I title match. I have fond memories of the Columbia Lions. Columbia's mascot lions are fierce, powerful, and, of course, the king of the jungle. But are lions resilient? They have a restricted diet that requires hunting with physical speed and strength. If they get injured or too old to perform, they quickly perish. On the other hand, consider a turtle. It lacks speed and elegance, but has few dietary restrictions. A turtle can swim fairly rapidly and hibernate in the extreme seasons. In times of danger, the turtle can snap its jaws and, in extreme danger, can retract into the armor of its hard shell and disappoint its predators. Turtles live a long time.

Grit and resilience are what I consider the most powerful traits a person, a team, or an organization can possess to predict future success.

40

Develop an improved surgical technique.

A universal goal that permeates skill acquisition is the need to command the skills required of a profession: to be better than competent. On a higher level, some will achieve mastery that, in fact, changes the profession. A career in surgery always appealed to me because of the ability to shape the evolution of new and fascinating developments. Paradigm shifts frequently occur in sports, music, and science. Someone comes along and changes the game. In table tennis, it was the introduction of a new grip; it was Impressionist painting in art. In surgery, it was the arthroscopic minimally invasive techniques that reduced pain, length of stay, and patient complications. In surgery, it is, in large part, individuals who change the game with the tools at their disposal. Names are given to procedures developed to reflect each surgeon's contribution (e.g., the Darrach Procedure, the Neer Capsular Shift, the Latarjet procedure).

When I was a fourth-year resident, an attending scheduled an arthroscopic lateral release[2] procedure for treatment of a young girl who was frequently dislocating her patella. A surgical outcome had been previously published indicating that lateral release (an operation simply to incise the tissue adjacent to the knee cap) was ineffective and had an extremely high failure rate. I questioned the procedure and poor results associated with it to the attending and he acknowledged it, but also indicated to me that he had offered an attractive minimally invasive arthroscopic surgery to the patient and family. I explained to the attending that all arthroscopic stabilization procedures indicated for the shoulder could be applied to the knee. We discussed it with the young patient's family and they agreed. Later that week, we executed the first arthroscopic patellar stabilization on this young girl, which had a successful result.

Look at opportunities in surgery to improve what exists. Get in the lab and reach and try. This does not always work, but talented surgeons are always thinking about what will be the next technical paradigm shift. Scientific creativity needs to be practiced and follows the same principles for skill development—finding the sweet spot, and reaching, and repeating. Surgery and medicine are complex. Like economics and agriculture, a multitude of factors influence and affect the system. Complex tasks will always have room for advancement. In, contrast the 100-meter dash has less opportunity for paradigm shifts because there are fewer variables.

Many surgeons will have an opportunity to create and pursue an advancement in the field during their career. Dr. Atul Gawande, an endocrine surgeon practicing at Massachusetts General Hospital, described the impact of a series of global healthcare improvements in his book *Better*. He recommended, in closing his book, that readers become a positive deviant. He suggested they start measuring something, anything. Once you have data, you can analyze and make adjustments to improve that particular situation. Many of the most famous talents we recognize not only broke records, but changed how we view their discipline. Steve Jobs' ambition and enormous creativity changed personal computing. I have stolen from him (Tip #4) when I say, "Let's make a dent in the Orthopaedic Universe."

Look for the opportunity to change the profession. Then change it.

PART FOUR:
ADDITIONAL REFLECTIONS

MANY OF THESE TIPS are clearly interrelated or interdependent. Consider skill acquisition and performance as a complex system, and the tips are the subsystems that interrelate. The next reflections are a "putting it all together" endeavor, so to speak, on specific topics and the interrelations of the different tips.

If he is such a good surgeon, why can't he operate?

Surgery is performed by people who often have a physical presence, like an athlete's presence on the playing field or Tiger Woods' intimidating red shirt on Sunday. Patients and staff can sense a surgeon's confidence. But surgeons do not live within statistical measures of performance, as opposed to a golfer who has average drive distance and percent fairways hits, or all the numbers that rate a baseball player on the back of a baseball card. In the movie *Moneyball*, Billy Beane employs new metrics to value baseball players and he questions his top scouts who are promoting prospects, "If he is such a good hitter, why can't he hit?"

Perceptions of great surgeons rely on numerous factors. So-called "bedside manner" most greatly influences patients' perceptions. These patients, in fact, frequently apologize to their surgeon when the surgical result is poor. Some skilled technical surgeons lack a bedside manner and interpersonal skills. If they experience an unfortunate complication, more of their patients don't hesitate to file a lawsuit. Some surgeons are nationally recognized because they are polished speakers and lecture well, like someone who could emcee the Academy Awards, yet their surgical skill and personal outcomes are weakly developed. Some surgeons advertise the number of surgeries they have done, as patients incorrectly equate this to skill. As we have outlined however, some do it poorly and do it a lot, but promote themselves well. Billy Beane in *Moneyball* developed new metrics and measures of what a player can contribute to a winning team—he created new definitions of value. We also need to better define and measure the value and skill of a surgeon. These new metrics—similar to on-base percentages, for example—then need to be used. We have paperwork for core competencies on surgery. Are residents getting better? We, as surgical teachers now can officially grade them and critique their performance.

The characteristics of a superior surgeon when compared to a weaker surgeon are elusive at times, but become easier to identify in stressful situations. This book has offered strategies to build skills and excellence and can, at some point, be incorporated into an official training platform. Next steps will be to determine the Sabermetrics[3] of a surgeon's value. (Sabermetrics is a baseball term that refers to a system that assigns value to a baseball player based on his performance and ability to contribute to his team winning.)

REFLECTION 2

Take a chess lesson. My 10-year-old son is an aspiring chess player who began playing before and after school with friends. He then started taking after-school group chess lessons. He loves it. He now has a private coach who sets up positions on the board, and then the game is played with black and then with white, and the positions are analyzed. We often analyze surgery in a similar way. Chess has infinite combinations as the game is played, similar to the infinite combinations of variables at play in surgery—for example, pathology, patient expectations, the activity levels of patients, the surgeon's comfort level, environmental factors, equipment, and anesthesia.

Chess players in training replay classic games to explore their beauty and instructive qualities. An example is the 'Opera Game' played by Paul Morphy vs. Carl Isouard Paris, 1858. This famous game demonstrates essential chess concepts such as rapid *development* and *forcing moves*. Students play this game over and over, memorizing each move. Each time they play it, they can push deeper into the concepts. The acquisition of a skill in a new surgical procedure requires you to revisit that procedure from beginning to end and then repeat it. When expertise with that singular surgery increases to a high level, the process of learning can then be applied to other procedures.

The chess model of learning influenced my Surgical Techniques Conference to train residents. This conference requires a selected resident to present and describe an actual surgery from beginning to end with photos illustrating every step. In the chess model, players examine a position (the board with pieces in position as played up until that point), decide their best perceived move, then compare that move to the moves of master players and analyze the differences. This creates high repetition of real life moves with immediate feedback. This is markedly superior to simply playing enjoyable games. This real practice is extremely powerful and can be employed in all fields, and particularly, to surgery.

Every Friday, at 6 a.m., one of my residents begins presenting a surgical case with PowerPoint. The surgery, usually performed earlier that week, is captured with photos. The surgical details start with how the patient is positioned: on his side with a roll in his axilla (armpit) and bean bag to support him. The resident continues until I interrupt and ask "What is the consequence if it's done differently?" In chess, when my son Charlie makes a move, the grandmaster then asks why and plays out the consequence, e.g., the queen can get trapped and then lost and then the game is over. A resident continues to present each step of surgery in sequence. Why place the retractor there? If it's left there too long and with too much pressure, what happens? Radial nerve palsy leading to a patient who can't lift his or her wrist up after distal biceps repair is one option. This resident will now avoid that complication. I ask questions to push them past their limits, to stretch their understanding of each component of the surgery.

Surgical case conference can be carried out in an intimidating way. It's so stressful, residents can get emotional. There is no place to hide and your abilities or lack of abilities are exposed to all in the audience. Fear of embarrassment can preclude growth for some. We had one resident who spent a huge amount of energy avoiding this conference. Somehow, the resident was always scheduled to be at another site and never got beat up in front of others. Years later, we discovered the resident quit being an orthopaedic surgeon.

Teaching is done differently today. Many residents value educational presentations where a master surgeon stands in front of them with a slide show and then walks them through the steps of making an accurate diagnosis of a shoulder fracture, which options to fix the fracture are best, how to choose the best implant to fix it, then how to put the plate on without damaging nerves and muscles. The residents are leisurely and passively engaged. There is a stimulating component to sitting and listening to an engaging speaker and seeing complex surgery and decision-making at its best. It relates to tip #1 to stare at those you admire. This, however, fails in what we now know about learning and excellence. There is no reaching during the presentation.

My tip is to never go to a lecture passively, no matter what. I write something down from any lecture or experience I attend, text myself the note, and then file it in my notebook. And then, I study my notebook at a later date.

Elite chess players are thought of as having incredibly high IQs and the ability to project moves into the future much better than average people. Research has shown that chess masters have very average IQs and their superior abilities are related to chunking. Consider the experiment in 1973 by William Chase and Herbert Simon, psychologists. Two groups: one consisting of chess masters, and the other composed of novices, are shown chessboards with 20 to 25 pieces for a brief moment. The groups are then asked to reconstruct the board. The novices are able to correctly place four to five pieces, but the masters can place them all accurately.

This seems to support the chess masters' superior memory and IQ. However, phase two of the experiment indicates otherwise. The groups were shown the boards, but the pieces were placed randomly and not consistent with true game situations. The experts and the novices were now no better at placing the pieces on the boards. Chess does not build increased memory power; it develops the process of chunking. Through the principles of skill acquisition, elite chess players have gained a mental library of themes and positions that as experts they can recognize and others can't.

The reason for this is pattern recognition. If the grandmaster can recall similar positions encountered in the past, the same themes and concepts might be applicable to the game in hand. This makes it much easier and quicker to analyze a position. It especially applies to the most basic attacking formations around the enemy king. Once a known motif is spotted, the moves of the optional combinations are analyzed to check that they do indeed work in the particular position on the board. It is clear then that chess analysis is a mixture of calculation of individual moves and pattern recognition.

Effectively, all chess players think in this way (consciously or otherwise!) however, the rationale between these two methods of thought is different for players of varying strengths. Although no scientific tests have been done, inexperienced players use perhaps 95 percent calculation and five percent pattern recognition. Logically, therefore, learning to recognize more key patterns could help dramatically improve your chess strength. Magnus Carlsen is currently the number one chess player in the world.

He played Bill Gates and beat him in one minute. He has been able to keep 10 games of chess going at once without even looking, and still win. Knowledge of patterns acquired by experts is so deep, their libraries so vast, they are able to create mental models of how a sequence of events should play out, and quickly—almost instantly—detect problems. Chess players at the masters' level, for instance, can play while blindfolded with only a minor reduction in their chess ability. Expert pianists are able to fix notational errors in music on the fly, automatically correcting the music back to what the genre would have predicted.

Many aspects of medical training resemble the chess model of learning. Residents take a patient's history, perform physicals, order and interpret tests, formulate a diagnosis and treatment plan. They then present the patient to an attending, who then repeats the process in front of the resident so they can learn from the style and observe where they deviated.

REFLECTION 3

Enhance surgical performance like a musical performance.

What does any elite performer do prior to an event, competition, or performance? He runs through his pregame routine. In sports, warming up involves getting blood flowing to muscles. Watch Lebron James warm up. He jogs, stretches, shoots. He is warming up his body and warming up his mind. Warm-ups generally consist of gradual increases in exercise intensity, some stretching, and activity-specific movements. This phase of the warm-up is to circulate the blood and warm the muscles in preparation for more strenuous activity, followed by stretching, followed by sport-specific activity—catching and throwing a basketball, for example. Musicians play scales before a performance. Chess players do tactics problems to get their mind flowing prior to the match. I regularly run the NYC marathon; I am on the bridge with the elites. I run alongside so and so. Pants are kept on so muscles get and stay warm. It is not until the game starts that stuff comes off. What is the purpose of warming up?

Better physical performance. Avoid injury. And yes—surgeons warm up mentally prior to the three to four hours of mental challenge they'll face in the operating room.

THE MIND BODY INTERACTION

Yogi Berra once said, "90 percent of this game is 50 percent mental." Football players do mental conditioning. How important is it? The University of Alabama has won three out of the last four BCS National Football Championships. For all three National Championships, Trevor Moawad has been their Mental Conditioning Coach. The assignment for the football Mental Conditioning Coach is the following: maximize teamwork, educational action, anticipation, motivation, leadership, communication, competitive spirit, and character to maximize on-field performance. Football Mental Conditioning Coordinators execute a series of pre-practice and pre-game activities, consisting of fewer than 10 minutes, to maximize practice performance and game day performance.

The Congress of Neurological Surgeons recently named Dr. Gazi Yasargil the Neurosurgeon of the Century. He has also been addressing the mental aspects of surgery beyond the technical. He regularly compares effective surgery to performing a symphony, and refers to his six-person operating team as "a sextet who must perform together like an orchestra."

How do surgeons enhance their surgical performance? Here is my routine. Three days before a big day of surgery, I review the operative indications, imaging studies, and make sure all necessary patient and surgery-specific issues are managed. The day before surgical day—I review all the imaging studies again and review the sequence of surgeries. I create the order of surgeries such that simple surgeries are done first, which serve as a warm-up for the more difficult ones later in the day. On the night before surgery—early carbohydrate meal, lots of hydration, mentally rehearse each sequence before going to sleep. The day of surgery—wake up early, on drive to hospital I again mentally rehearse the select surgeries I believe to be most difficult for that day. I get to the hospital and begin by directing our surgical technique conference. This conference reviews and analyzes specific surgical techniques and further starts my warm-up for the day. I see my first patients at 7 a.m. and obtain surgical consent from them to undergo the procedure. I then meet the anesthesia staff and OR staff. Go through a huddle and discuss any aspects of the day that are not routine. Surgery begins at 8 a.m. I typically operate from 8 a.m. to 5 p.m., but sometimes 8 p.m. After surgery, I write down the grades I give to myself and debrief with myself on the potential areas to improve for the next day of surgery.

REFLECTION 4

Don't choke. Some surgeons resemble elite athletes who perform with extraordinary ability in the face of extreme pressure and rise above the anxieties and doubts that so often paralyze lesser performers. They retain the sureness of touch, their subtlety of mind, all those deep and complex motor skills built up over thousands of hours. Other surgeons melt under extreme pressure.

How do we explain poor performance that relates to pressure? Robert Gray at Arizona State University took elite baseball players and asked them to swing at a moving ball while listening to tones of different frequencies and instructed them to judge whether the tone was high or low. There were no negative effects on their swing during this exercise. When hitters were asked to indicate whether their bat was moving up or down at the instant the tone sounded, their performance level plunged. Explicit monitoring of their performance destroyed their performance.

The problem was not lack of focus, but too much focus. Conscious monitoring disrupted the smooth working of the automated unconscious system. The sequencing and timing of the different motor responses became fragmented, regressing their process to that of a novice. They are, effectively, beginners again. This explains golfers suffering from the so called "yips," which is the result of trying to monitor their putting stroke. Choking is a problem of psychological reversion: The automation and unconscious effort to execute the skill works, but when deconstructed, because of anxiety, can cause disastrous failure. Why do coaches call a time out before their opponents execute a game-winning free throw opportunity? Initiating choking by creating time for the shooter to think may interfere and deconstruct the natural automated throw.

Another type of choking stems from negative framing. For example, a golfer lining up a putt should tell herself, "Center of the stroke," not, "Don't pull this putt to the left." A violinist faced with a difficult passage should tell himself: "Nail that A-flat." not "Oh boy, I hope I don't miss that A-flat." Psychologists call this "positive framing." It always works better to reach for what you want to accomplish, not resist what you want to avoid.

A positive mindset and positive framing is essential in surgery. If, in a complex case, the surgeon is too nervous and concentrates on avoiding a mistake during execution, the surgery fails to execute well. A fine balance exists between confidence and recognizing potential problems and avoiding them with maintenance of positive thoughts versus negative, fearful thinking. The destructive effects escalate if, in fact, your biggest fear starts to happen. For example, if your dissection is tentative to avoid bleeding because you have an extreme fear of bleeding and then bleeding occurs, your ability to react and manage the bleeding is poor. A positive mindset can be critical during vital surgical moments. To build a positive mindset, I practice by visualizing complications during surgery prior, and then, literally, tell myself, "This is the most opportune time to help my patient." I create a positive mindset where I look forward to intra-operative crises so I can demonstrate confidence and manage it. I set a mindset where I believe I have prepared and can overcome anything.

We have all choked in some environment. On his website, Dan Coyle describes a terrifying pressure experiment performed by a Harvard professor Alison Wood Brooks, the *ambush-style karaoke*. A group of volunteers were brought together. They were then surprised by informing them that they were to solo the first verse of Journey's "Don't Stop Believing." A short time before they performed, subjects were told to repeat one of three phrases out loud.

1) *I am calm.*

2) *I am anxious.*

3) *I am excited.*

Voice-recognition software measured the quality of their vocal performance—pitch, volume, and rhythm. The results: "I am calm" performers scored 53 percent, "I am anxious" performers scored 69 percent, and "I am excited" performers scored 81 percent. The explanation is that mantras functioned as psychological framing devices. The "I am calm" group performed poorly because the words denied the reality of the situation. Their words claimed they weren't nervous. The disparity created tension, so their performance suffered.

The "I am anxious" group told the truth, but in an ineffective way. The negativity was damaging. The "I am excited" group performed best because the frame was both useful and accurate. They acknowledged the heightened emotion of the situation and funneled it in a positive direction. It wasn't the truth, exactly, but it was aligned with the truth, and thus proved useful in dampening nerves and enabling better performance. "When your heart is already racing, you can use that high arousal in a positive way by being energetic, enthusiastic, and passionate," Brooks says. "People's intuition is to try and calm down. You are better off running with your high arousal and channeling it in a positive direction." For us, I think the lessons are useful.

In his song, "Lose Yourself," Eminem powerfully captures the body-wide physical and emotional meltdown that too-often occurs when you're confronted with your one shot at everything you ever wanted and how horribly—and quickly—it can go awry.

Panic, in this sense, is the opposite of choking. Choking is about thinking too much. Panic is about thinking too little. Choking is about loss of instinct. Panic is reversion to instinct. They may look the same, but are far from it. John F. Kennedy Jr.'s tragic plane crash in July 1999 has been ascribed to panic. Kennedy has limited visibility as he was trying to pick up the lights of Martha's Vineyard. He began a path of turns and then a rapid descent into the Atlantic Ocean. The National Transportation Safety Board (NTSB) determined the crash was caused by "the pilot's failure to maintain control of the airplane during a descent over water at night, which was a result of spatial disorientation." If he were choking, he would have gone back to the mechanical, self-conscious application of the lessons he had first received as a pilot—and that might have been a good thing. Kennedy needed to think, to concentrate on his instruments, to break away from the instinctive flying that served him when he had a visible horizon. Unfortunately he panicked.

I heard of a surgeon who was operating on a patient with an intertrochanteric hip fracture. The procedure involved placing a plate with a large screw into the hip to fix it into proper position and with strength to allow the patient to begin walking immediately after surgery. This is a basic procedure for all orthopaedic surgeons. While the plate was being applied, the bone of the femur crumbled into several pieces. The plate could no longer be used to fix the problem. What now? The surgeon simply left the operating room without saying anything. The assisting resident was left to manage the complex, difficult situation alone. The attending surgeon was overwhelmed. The surgeon panicked. Panic resorts to basic instinct. Stress wipes out short-term memory. People with lots of experience tend not to panic, because when the stress suppresses their short-term memory, they still have some residue of experience to draw on.

My friends growing up in high school called the guy who made the last out in our summer whiffle ball contests "Chokey" for the rest of the day and sometimes even longer. This term describes a very specific kind of failure. Under conditions of stress, however, the explicit system sometimes takes over. That's what it means to choke. Chuck Knoblauch, the New York Yankees' second baseman, inexplicably, has had trouble throwing the ball to first base. Under the stress of playing in front of 40,000 fans at Yankee Stadium, Knoblauch finds himself reverting to explicit mode, throwing like a Little Leaguer again.

I have residents observe me when I perform knee arthroscopy while I explain the technique of making a 5mm incision, introducing a blunt obturator, placing the camera, then taking four initial pictures. Up, left, right, down. I tell them to study this. It has the complexity of ordering a skinny vanilla latte at Starbucks. They can recite to me that they will cut the skin, insert the obturator, place the camera and take the pictures—up, left, right down. When I give residents the scalpel for the first time, I look them in the eye and usually say something like "Here is your shot at the title, kid."

It has been rare for a resident to perform well with a first attempt despite the low complexity of the task. They usually fail at the point of taking pictures when they start taking pictures of anything that moves. Why? Great question. I even tell them right before I give them the scalpel that no resident has ever done the four simple photos correctly. With the scalpel comes a rush of adrenaline. They draw a blank. This is choking, but with limited consequence.

Choking is a central part of the drama of athletic competition, because the spectators have to be there, and the ability to overcome the pressure of the spectators is part of what it means to be a champion. But the same ruthless inflexibility need not govern the rest of our lives. We have to learn that sometimes a poor performance reflects not the innate ability of the performer but the complexion of the audience; and that sometimes a poor test score is the sign, not of a poor student, but of a good one.

Greg Norman was nicknamed "The Shark." He had a blonde-haired appearance of invincibility and is well known for one of the greatest chokes in sports history. Through the first three rounds of the 1996 Masters Golf Tournament, Norman held a comfortable lead over his nearest rival, the Englishman Nick Faldo. Norman was paired with Faldo for the final day. At the ninth hole, Norman swung and then froze, his club in midair, following the ball in flight. It was short. Norman watched, stone-faced, as the ball rolled 30 yards back down the hill, and, with that error, something inside of him broke.

At the 10th hole, he hooked the ball to the left, hit his third shot well past the cup, and missed a makeable putt. At 11, Norman had a three-and-a-half-foot putt for par—the kind he had been making all week. He shook out his hands and legs before grasping the club, trying to relax. He missed: his third straight bogey. At 12, Norman hit the ball straight into the water. At 13, he hit it into a patch of pine needles. At 16, his movements were so mechanical and out of synch that, when he swung, his hips spun out ahead of his body and the ball sailed into another pond. At that, he took his club and made a frustrated scythe-like motion through the grass, because what had been obvious for 20 minutes was now official: he had fumbled away the chance of a lifetime.

Faldo had begun the day six strokes behind Norman. By the time the two started their slow walk to the 18th hole, through the throng of spectators, Faldo had a four-stroke lead. But he took those final steps quietly, giving only the smallest of nods, keeping his head low. He understood what had happened on the greens and fairways that day. And he was bound by the particular etiquette of choking, the understanding that what he had earned was something less than a victory, and what Norman had suffered was something less than a defeat.

When it was all over, Faldo wrapped his arms around Norman. "I don't know what to say—I just want to give you a hug," he whispered, and then he said the only thing you can say to a choker: "I feel horrible about what happened. I'm so sorry." With that, the two men began to cry.

Dan Coyle argues that proper preparation can be the difference in game day performance. In his experience, top performers make a habit of *pre-creating* pressure situations in vivid detail, so that when the time comes, they're ready and have less performance anxiety, fear, and choke potential. As an example, concert musicians use performance practice. They simulate the precise conditions (same formal clothes, same chair, sometimes even the same auditorium) and run through their program exactly as if it's opening night. Many sports teams routinely rehearse the last moments of games, piping in crowd noise, and increase the tempo beyond what they might see in a game. Special Forces soldiers spend virtually all of their training inside a pre-created, live-ammo, high-pressure world—not to break them, but rather to accustom them to it. Derek Jeter has been one of the most mentally locked-in athletes of our century. As a high school sophomore, he hit a three pointer to win a basketball game and has never doubted his ability to perform under pressure until the final game of his career. Surgeons similarly require extreme mental confidence.

REFLECTION 5

Coaching. Being good at whatever you do—running marathons, performing magic tricks, taking great photos, baking cakes—is among the greatest sensations of deep fulfillment we will ever know. I've been an orthopaedic surgeon for 12 years. While I pushed my strategies to acquire surgical skill in various ways, I also encountered numerous performance plateaus along the journey. In the first two or three years in practice, my skills and confidence improved continuously, the steep and satisfying part of the learning curve was also accompanied by uneasiness knowing I was on the low end of the curve.

As I achieved surgical mastery in my later years, I began to utilize deeper judgment, applied my experiences and relied much less on the hard skills of so-called "good hands." In reality, the skills possessed by the most talented surgeons are, in many ways, measured in variables that are elusive. We need those same Sabermetrics that changed baseball for physicians and surgeons, and institutions of medical care.

Surgery became a platform of mastered hard skills with low-growth velocity combined with soft skills that maintained higher-growth velocity. Soft skills grow with accumulating experience. "Experience is what you get when you didn't get what you wanted. And experience is often the most valuable thing you have to offer," said Randy Pausch in his moving *Last Lecture*. The path to higher-level achievement is tough. If you are green, you are growing; if you are ripe, you are close to rotten. When you stop your quest, your growth ceases.

As I am writing this, I am also thinking about tomorrow, where I am treating a college pitcher who blew out his elbow, one of the conditions I treat as an expert in baseball medicine. We have a celebrated solution: Tommy John surgery, which has predictable results, but a lengthy recovery. A 10cm incision is made. A graft is taken from the wrist. The forearm muscles are separated to expose the damaged ligament. Small tunnels creating sockets are drilled on both bones comprising the elbow joint. The graft is weaved through these bony sockets and sewn into place. The muscles that were dissected to achieve exposure are repaired, the skin is closed, and a brace is applied.

But before this patient makes it to the operating room, an amazing set of judgments and integrated mental analysis took place. Many are related to snap judgments or chunked information acquired over many years. Is the diagnosis accurate; can the injury heal on its own without surgery; are the patient's expectations correct; is he interested in surgery simply to improve performance; does he have a pitching flaw causing the problem in the first place; are there associated injuries that need to be addressed such as bone spurs in the back of the elbow?

My improvisational soft skills have somewhat plateaued since I feel I have rehearsed every possible complication and problem that could arise and have algorithms in place for solutions. I have found deep gratification from those patients who returned to the highest levels of competition. Recently, I learned one of my patients was drafted by the Yankees, and I will be doing a contract physical exam to attest to his health durability. I am also troubled by those athletes I have treated who did not achieve their full potential. Still, my personal results are favorable to those reported in the literature.

I recently completed my "Maintenance of Certification" exam. This is required of all orthopaedic surgeons to maintain their board certification status. It's a highly criticized process, with those in opposition arguing that a single multiple choice test cannot assess the competence of an experienced surgeon. I studied some questions and went to a computer testing center in Manhattan and sat for three hours reading and answering questions. I passed the test. I have been asked by the American Orthopaedic Society for Sports Medicine to lecture at a review course they give for upcoming test takers. Studying and taking the test did not enhance my skill in orthopaedic surgery. In fact, it did not make me any more competent or help me assess my own competency. (In fact, it was an opportunity cost in that I could have devoted the practice time to an actual increase in surgical competence.)

As a surgeon with a desire for continued growth and maintaining the steepness of my growth curve, and with the tools of self-reflection, honest feedback, and deep practice styles, I have tried to get clever with new approaches. My greatest learning experiences now come from small discussions with other talented surgeons, often the ones with gray hair. I seek them out at meetings and present them with difficult situations and ask them what they would do. I recently moderated an elbow surgery instructional course and presented cases to the faculty in front of a large audience and asked them "What would you do?" After the session, I took copious notes despite the fact that I was the intended instructor.

Skill and talent plateaus in many settings. My personal experience with soccer, and my experience providing care for elite professional baseball players, suggest to me that athletic skills tend to plateau early in relative age and career. Athletes with a predilection for pure hard skills often peak earlier. People with a predilection for soft skills, such as those who run companies, often peak later. In fact, research shows that many CEOs and Nobel Prize winners are older compared to those from decades ago. My soccer career peaked in college and now is almost a purely spectator opportunity for me; my chess career, however, is just beginning.

Young, talented chess players have coaches. The most elite chess players who achieve the highest ratings such as grandmaster status most often do not. They graduate into an arena where they work on their own. Coaching in sports requires someone who sees athletes in a way that they can't see themselves and then gives them feedback. The coaches also possess talents for relating to the student or athlete and observing weaknesses that can be targeted for improvement. I have been taking chess lessons from a grandmaster, or GM, as they are called. This GM during his youth regularly studied openings into the night and early mornings and, by age 14, he had a rating of 2400 (which is ridiculously high). Such an experienced chess coach sees moves you are unable see yourself, can point them out to you, and also can point out what the opponent is trying to do that you can't see on your own.

So a surgeon observing another surgeon is like a pitcher watching another pitcher during a game. He can pick up some things, but it is not the same as having a pitching coach. The pitching coach for the Yankees busily fine-tunes all aspects of the pitchers' mechanics. In addition, the pitchers have a massage therapist to keep their muscles relaxed prior to pitching, have a mental conditioning coach to ensure they are mentally prepared, a strength and conditioning coach to make sure they are physically optimized. Surgeons do not have the equivalent of these coaches. The features of exceptional coaches are the subject of numerous discussions, great books, and movies.

Atul Gawande, a general surgeon from Harvard, recognized the lack of coaching in his own pursuit of surgical excellence. Gawande launched an experiment working with a surgery coach (*Personal Best,* by Atul Gawande, October 3, 2011). He enlisted a retired surgeon whose career he wished to emulate. Gawande described his coach as a surgical attending who strained to get residents to think like surgeons, who asked frequent questions to expose how much learning remained. His coach came to his operating room and observed his surgery.

After surgery, he pointed out things he saw that Gawande could not see himself: the patient was draped in a way that compromised his surgical assistant across the table. He also observed that Gawande's right elbow was elevated to the level of his shoulder, compromising consistent and precise movements. He observed his failure to keep tissue under tension. Gawande's coach made an interesting and pointed remark. "Most surgery is done in your head. Your performance is not determined by where you stand or where your elbow goes. It's determined by where you decide to stand, where you decide to put your elbow."

In medicine, there is little mentorship once surgeons are done with residency. In fact, you are lucky if you get an annual review from your boss. Maintaining your board certification is done with a multiple choice exam test. You study for the test, take the test, pass the test, but have not improved your care of patients in any way. Perhaps the best reason to have a coach is to have an observer point out your mistakes.

We often spend our time teaching principles of surgery rather than principles of learning, such as deep practice with feedback and focused repetition. We are neglecting and, even, robbing our young surgical minds of achievement and believe that we are doing well by instituting paperwork to evaluate core competencies. We may even give occasional feedback with strengths and weaknesses, but we do not teach how to practice and take self-control of a future quest for excellence.

Moving forward, a goal of surgical education will be to impart the practice of skill acquisition and performance strategy.

———————

REFLECTION 6

Patients entrust their safety and out-come to you.
Motivation to take the difficult road to mastery is elusive. In medicine, the patient is a major motivational feature. Therefore, I often get discouraged when a resident fails to prepare well for a case. Reasons for lack of preparation abound; they're tired or disinterested. The privilege that patients give to their surgeon to operate on them is one of the most honorable positions and responsibilities a person with a job description can have. The patient entrusts their body to you. For many residents, this is not respected appropriately. The resident can recite the Krebs cycle, yet does not know the anatomy of the ulnar nerve when assisting on a MCL reconstruction; does not know that the major complication of the surgery is an injury to the ulnar nerve and this can be minimized with simple preparation and review of the nerve anatomy and techniques to avoid nerve injury. I explain to my residents that their role in assisting in every surgery is a true test of their

life mission and, if they studied less for each surgery than they did in college for tests on forgot-
ten subjects, then they failed the trust of their
patient who believes in them. Never lose sight of
your immense responsibility, which can be in any
field or position.

FINAL MESSAGE

Why is the profession of medicine referred to as medical practice? I do not know the answer but I do know that in all fields, disciplines, and professions, individuals have room for growth, and mastery is reachable using proven principles. The difference between expert performers and the rest of the world reflects a life-long passion and deliberate effort to improve performance in a specific domain. The path is clear, long and demanding—few will follow it. Everyone who has achieved skill has encountered terrible difficulties along the way; there are no exceptions.

END NOTES

1   **Tommy John Surgery.** Tommy John surgery is a surgical graft procedure in which the ulnar collateral ligament in the medial elbow is replaced with a tendon from elsewhere in the body. The procedure is common among collegiate and professional athletes in several sports, most notably baseball. The procedure was first performed in 1974 by orthopaedic surgeon Dr. Frank Jobe, then a Los Angeles Dodgers team physician who served as a special advisor to the team until his death in 2014. It is named after the first baseball player to undergo the surgery, former major league pitcher Tommy John, whose 288 career victories ranks seventh all time among left-handed pitchers. The surgery involves an incision and open exploration of the damaged ligament. Holes are created to form sockets to accommodate a new tendon in the ulna and humerus bones of the elbow. A harvested tendon (often the palmaris tendon from the forearm of the same or opposite elbow or the gracilis tendon from the knee) is then woven through the holes and anchored. While the surgery takes one hour, the recovery takes a full year.

2   **Lateral release procedure.** The lateral release is a surgical procedure to release tight, capsular structures (lateral retinaculum) on the outer aspect (lateral aspect) of the kneecap (patella). This is usually

performed because of knee pain related to the knee-cap being pulled over to the outer (lateral) side and not tracking properly in the groove of the femur bone as the knee bends and straightens. Amongst experienced knee surgeons with a special interest in diseases of the patellofemoral articulation, isolated lateral release is rarely performed and not generally indicated as an isolated procedure to solve the problem of a dislocating patella. Strong consensus was found that isolated lateral release should not be undertaken without prior planning in the form of objective clinical indications and preoperative informed consent.

3   **Sabermetrics.** Sabermetrics is the term for the empirical analysis of baseball, especially baseball statistics that measure in-game activity. The term is derived from the acronym SABR, which stands for the Society for American Baseball Research. It was coined by Bill James, one of its pioneers. Sabermetricians frequently question traditional measures of baseball skill. For instance, they doubt that batting average is as useful as conventional wisdom says it is because team batting average provides a relatively poor fit for team runs scored. Sabermetric reasoning would say that runs win ballgames, and that a good measure of a player's value is his ability to help his team score more runs than the opposing team. This may imply that the traditional RBI (runs batted in) is an effective metric; however, sabermetricians also reject RBI, for a number of reasons. Rather, sabermetric measures are usually phrased in terms of either runs or team wins. For example, a player might be described as being worth 54 offensive runs more than a replacement-level player at the same position during the course of a full season, as the sabermetric statistic VORP can indicate.

ACKNOWLEDGEMENTS

I would like to sincerely thank and acknowledge those who have shaped my education, enhanced my professional skill, and steered the direction of my journey.

James R. Andrews

Louis U. Bigliani

James P. Bradley

Brian J. Cole

John E. Conway

Neal S. ElAttrache

Evan L. Flatow

Jack H. Henry

Frank W. Jobe

William N. Levine

Bert R. Mandelbaum

Peter J. Millet

Anthony A. Romeo

Melvin P. Rosenwasser

Felix H. Savoie, III

Reinhold Schmieding

Beth E. Shubin Stein

James E. Tibone

Michael G. Vitale

Lewis A. Yocum

NOTES

ABOUT CHRISTOPHER S. AHMAD, MD

Christopher S. Ahmad, MD is the Head Team Physician for the New York Yankees and a member of the Major League Baseball Team Physicians Association. He is also a Professor of Orthopaedic Surgery at the Columbia University College of Physicians and Surgeons and an Attending Orthopaedic Surgeon at the New York-Presbyterian/Columbia University Medical Center.

Dr. Ahmad grew up in Long Island with a passion for playing soccer and played in the New York Empire State Games, the Eastern Region Olympic Development Team, and four years of varsity soccer at the nationally ranked Columbia University. His background in soccer stimulated his career path that is dedicated to the treatment and prevention of youth sports injuries.

He currently serves as the Chief of Sports Medicine and as the Director of Biomechanics Research at the Center for Orthopaedic Research. He has authored more than 100 articles and book chapters related to knee, shoulder, elbow, and sports medicine, and has given more than 100 lectures nationally and internationally.

He is the author of the textbooks *Pediatric and Adolescent Sports Injuries* and *Minimally Invasive Shoulder and Elbow Surgery*. Dr. Ahmad has received many awards for outstanding research in the field of sports medicine.

Dr. Ahmad has served on MLB research committees to address the high incidence of Tommy John Surgeries in professional baseball. He is also the Head Team Physician for the new expansion Major League Soccer New York City Football Club and for local high schools and serves as consultant to local metropolitan gymnastics and swim teams.

CPSIA information can be obtained
at www.ICGtesting.com
Printed in the USA
BVHW040253100623
665686BV00007B/256